14.97

Foolproof
Finances
Financial
Survival
from the
Bible

by David Mallonee

Kingdom™
Mansfield, Pennsylvania

Kingdom, Inc.
Lambs Creek Road   phone: 1-800-334-1456
P. O. Box 486   phone: 717-662-7515
Mansfield, PA 16933   fax: 717-662-3875
internet: http://www.kingdominc.com/

As the founder of Concepts in Stewardship, a teaching ministry dedicated to training the Body of Christ in finances, David Mallonee travels extensively throughout North America teaching the principles found in this book. If your church or organization would like to host a financial seminar by author David Mallonee, you may reach him by contacting his publisher, Kingdom, Inc. Feel free to write David Mallonee c/o Kingdom, Inc. He would be very pleased to hear how this book has affected your life.

First Edition

Acknowledgments

A project of this size cannot be accomplished alone. I want to thank the following people for their input into this book. I am indebted to these individuals for their encouragement, prayers, financial assistance, wisdom, and patience.

My wife, Nancy,
our two sons, Chris and Nathan,
and many friends including
Mark McIntosh,
Clay and Tracy Sikes,
and Dale Jacknitsky

Foolproof Finances

Contents

Other Titles by David Mallonee

Why Starve to Death in A Supermarket: The Biblical Road to Increasing Your Finances
The eight tape audio series
The eight lesson video series

Our prayer is that God will use this book to play a significant role in altering the course of your life financially. To order the audio series, the video series, or other products, please contact:

Kingdom, Inc.
Lambs Creek Road   phone: 1-800-334-1456
P. O. Box 486   phone: 717-662-7515
Mansfield, PA 16933   fax: 717-662-3875
       internet: http://www.kingdominc.com/

My Suggestions for Reading this Book

Like most people reading this book, I'm sure you have a desire to see your finances improve and to be a good steward of the resources God has entrusted to you. Perhaps, you would even like to see your entire financial situation turn around. I've seen dramatic turnarounds in the finances of numerous individuals as God transforms their heart and they start applying the principles found in this book. Or perhaps you are doing very, very well financially and as a good steward you want to do even better.

Before reading this book, I suggest you pray and ask God to show you His will for your finances. It is my prayer that this book will play a significant role in altering the course of your life financially. Then, read this book in its entirety. You don't have to read it all at once. After your first reading, go back and prayerfully start applying the principles chapter by chapter.

It would also be beneficial to find someone else who is also interested in improving their finances and go through the book with them. To go one step further, teach someone else the Biblical principles you are learning. Perhaps, you know someone who needs help getting their finances straightened out. Maybe you could offer some assistance. (Perhaps, you could even teach your kids.) Studies have indicated that if you teach something to someone else, you learn much better yourself. And of course then it will be easier to apply these principles because you'll thoroughly know them.

If you're extremely motivated and interested in improving *your* finances, perhaps you could start a small group study on finances. This would be very helpful. Just imagine the potential impact on not only your own finances, but the impact on the finances of people you know.

So, go ahead and prayerfully read this book.

Sincerely,
David Mallonee

Foreword by Johnny Berguson, President of Kingdom, Inc., one of America's 500 Fastest Growing Companies[1]

I am one of the many people whose financial turnaround parallels the principles in this book. This is the best financial teaching I've ever heard. I've used these principles for years, but I've never seen them explained. God has blessed me beyond belief and I give Him all the glory as I tell you the following story.

Years ago, I traveled as an evangelist with a performing horse. People knew us as "Johnny and the Sheik." As my Arabian horse and I traveled throughout the U.S. and Canada, thousands of men, women, and children came to faith in the Lord Jesus. We presented our program at small churches with only 14 present and in larger settings such as exhibitions with 30,000 in attendance. We appeared at events including rodeos, fairs, horse shows, and even the U.S. Arabian National Championship Horse Show. Four times we appeared on "The 700 Club" in addition to numerous other national television appearances. Many magazine articles, both secular and Christian, featured us. From all outward indicators, the road ahead was established and our future secure.

Suddenly, in one week's time, our itinerary collapsed. Cancellation after cancellation, all for different reasons, zeroed out our schedule for the remainder of the year. My wife and I were devastated and confused.

---

[1] Kingdom Company has been listed in *Inc. Magazine* as one of America's 500 fastest-growing privately held companies.

I prayed and prayed, but received no answers from the Lord. All I knew was that I needed to go to work. The Bible says, "If anyone will not work, neither shall he eat" (II Thessalonians 3:10). I looked daily for employment but, strangely, I could not find any durable job that would support my young and growing family.

The Lord impressed me with the verse, "In all labor there is profit" (Proverbs 14:23), so I decided to pursue an unusual idea. I would distribute audio cassettes on horse training. To train Sheik and other horses, I had applied Biblical principles for child rearing. They worked! I borrowed $500 on a credit card and started selling audio cassettes on horse training. The Lord blessed it. Over time it grew into a multi-million dollar enterprise.

Today, sixteen years later, Kingdom, Inc. still sells the 14 tape series entitled, "The World's Most Complete Course in Horse Training." Out of this endeavor grew a division called Kingdom Tapes, which supplies blank cassettes and electronics to churches all over the world. Today we also have Kingdom Computers, a division which assembles and distributes our own brand of personal computers. Our digital-audio studio, video-production company, printing company, and many other resources are each intended to serve the kingdom of God. All of this grew from the $500 which God blessed.

Not by Chance

This transformation did not happen by chance. Nor did God accomplish it instantly. I lived in relative poverty for years, but I always had enough. I did not want to set a price on preaching the Gospel, so I went to almost any place that invited us, whether it paid the bills for us or not. My focus then and now has been to "seek first the kingdom of God and his righteousness," believing He will take care of "all these things" (Matthew 6:33).

Let me offer a few specific examples of God's blessing. Before I started the horse ministry, I laid out a Gideon's fleece (see Judges 6). I said, "Lord, if you want me to do this, please provide me with a purebred Arabian horse. If not, don't let me get one." Within three weeks, Bazy Tankersley of Al-Marah Arabians gave me a purebred Arabian horse whose half-brother was valued at $80,000! This gift came in exchange for six shows I would do with the horse after I had trained him.

Al-Marah Majestic Sheik and I spent many memorable years participating in God's great faithfulness. Once my 22-year-old horse truck broke down, but we were directly in front of a horse farm. The proprietors rented us a horse trailer for $25. We also found a car we could borrow for free. As a result, we made the 600-mile trip on time and without further snags.

The day before our next trip, the president of Hartman Trailer Manufacturing Company gave me a 28-foot horse trailer. This generous gift had no strings attached. Here was a Jewish businessman who listened as I witnessed of my faith in Jesus Christ. A few minutes later something— or some One—moved this man to give me that wonderful trailer.

Not Always from God

Not all opportunities for prosperity are from the Lord, however. For example, one year my family was living with just enough to get by. Juanita, my wife, became very animated one morning. "I have just seen something in the Scriptures that we're not doing," she said. "We're not visiting people in prison." She showed me Hebrews 13:3.

I replied, "Yes, but we don't know anyone in prison." We agreed to ask the Lord to show us somebody we could visit.

The next day Juanita opened the mail and came running to me. It contained an unexpected letter from a man in a maximum-security prison. He had seen us on television and successfully found our address. He said he had $25,000 in his prison bank account that he wanted to give to us. He had another $25,000 that he wanted us to use to help his daughter and certain other people in need.

Soon we went to visit him. He offered us not $25,000, but $200,000! He had one condition, however. We had to dig up and distribute $400,000 he had buried prior to his incarceration. We listened to his elaborate and believable story about how the money got there. Certainly nothing was illegal about finding money in the ground, unless I knew it was connected with a crime, which I did not. Nevertheless, I felt certain in my heart that the money was "unclean." So we turned down the money and continued to trust God for our future.

By sticking with God's principles, any form of increase has come in His way and in His timing. For example, our business, Kingdom Tapes, has become one of the world's largest distributors of high-speed cassette duplicators. When Sony wanted to introduce their line of duplicators to the church market, they sent a representative to talk with me. He said Sony would like us to be one of five U.S. master distributors for their line. Thanks to God's prospering of us, we could have afforded to meet their requirements of an opening order for $30,000. However, I told Sony that I do not work that way. I've always tried to take a little and increase it. Proverbs 13:11 (NIV) says, "He who gathers money little by little makes it grow." I offered to buy one machine. I said that when I sold that one, I would buy more; I do not buy a lot of a new product that I have never sold. Sony agreed. Within months we were regularly placing orders of $30,000 or more. As of this writing, sales totals from our Sony line combined with our other brands of high-speed cassette duplicators put us at the top of the distribution charts.

All this multiplication occurred because we wanted to help churches have effective cassette ministries. In addition, each step of the way, we stuck with what we believed to be God's principles of finance.

Not too Quickly

As *Foolproof Finances* points out, you can change your money stream. Money can flow to you powerfully rather than away from you. But, it takes time to turn into God's flow. For instance, after I had been ministering part-time with my horse, my wife Juanita and I sensed that God wanted us to go full-time into this evangelistic ministry. We decided to move in with my parents for three months until "Johnny and the Sheik" could become fully self-supporting. It turned out that we could not afford to move out for three and a half years!

Turning into God's flow also cannot occur without faith-driven action. I remember one time when Juanita was having trouble trusting God for our finances. Her fears came to a head when I received a speeding ticket. All who know me, especially my wife and children, are aware that I do not intentionally speed. To this day, their teasing still will not persuade me to inch above the speed limit. Ironically, I had been driving uphill and was praying so hard—about our finances—that I exceeded the limit by 10 m.p.h. The radar gun caught me and the police officer issued a $70 ticket. We did not have the money to pay it. On the day the fine was due, I had to borrow the money. Juanita had expected the Lord to provide by that date. This experience shook Juanita's faith for a very short period of time.

Even my brothers and sisters began asking, "Johnny, what will you do if this horse evangelism doesn't work out?" I replied, "This is what the Lord has told me to do; I must keep following it until the Lord shows me something different."

The next morning, the Lord showed me that I needed to trust Him in new ways. In addition, Juanita resolved, "Lord, I don't understand why You didn't provide the $70, but I will trust you anyway." Later that day we received three phone invitations, two of which turned out to be 25,000-plus attendances, our largest live audiences to date. Yet the week before we could not even book ourselves into a small-town Fourth-of-July celebration! By the end of that week we had ten new invitations. We wound up the year in November at Central Gospel Temple, St. Catherine's,

Ontario, as 4,663 people came out to a Sunday-school promotion. This more than double-than-expected turnout capped a banner year where God had provided consistently far beyond our imaginations.

God's Money Stream

Following the principles outlined in this book by David Mallonee (rhymes with *PAL-oh-knee*), God has prospered us beyond belief. I am not saying everyone will increase in the same way as I did, but I have seen many of these truths work time and time again in my own life. I never pieced it all together the way David has phrased everything in this book.

In the process of coming to know David Mallonee personally, I have seen his integrity as he applies these teachings to his life. One instance involved a company charging him far more than what normal costs would be. Specialists in the field confirmed that he was being assessed double the going rate. Instead of fighting these people and bringing possible harm to the name of Christ (I Corinthians 6:1-8), he paid the bill in full because he believed that's what God wanted him to do in this situation.

I believe the Lord caused me to meet David Mallonee. As we became acquainted, I became very excited because the things he shared explained how God had worked in my life. In fact, I was so impressed with this material and with David Mallonee that I decided we needed to publish his book. It is the inaugural imprint in our new publishing division. We are also developing his materials in audiocassette and videocassette formats.

You may ask, are there not exceptions to the principles David outlines in this book? I realize the Scriptures speak of those "of whom the world was not worthy" (Hebrews 11:38), people like the Lord Jesus who had "nowhere to lay His head" (Matthew 8:20). Exceptions could include anything from nuclear war to persecution to certain other calamities the Lord allows. However, the person who follows these principles *will* prosper because that is the way God has set up the world. I sincerely believe you can prosper too.

I cannot recommend this book more heartily.

Johnny Berguson,
President of Kingdom, Inc.

Chapter 1

Why This Book?

"Pastor, I am a tither; I am a giver. But what the Bible says should be happening in my finances and what is really happening are two different things!"

"Brother David, I want to ask you about this tithing thing. Does it have to build up to a certain dollar amount before God begins to do anything?"

The concepts of this book took root during an eight-year period when I was pastoring a church in Missouri. I was certain God wanted to bless His people in every area, including their finances. Yet, I also could tell that something was missing.

These believers knew God cannot lie. Their perplexity arose because experience did not seem to square with the promises of Scripture. I assured them, along with others who asked similar questions, that God knows our hearts and our needs. We are not required to run through a probationary or pre-qualifying waiting time. He wants us to understand and experience His principles of increase as soon as we are able.

Over my years as a Christian, the Bible has painted in my mind a clear picture of Biblical increase. Although many of the Scriptures I encountered primarily address God's love, salvation, and other spiritual matters, I heard in them promises and principles which I believe can be applied to money and finances. In my study of the Old Testament, I have noted many pledges that God made to His people. Malachi 3:10, for example, contains a powerful promise about tithing. "'Try me now in this,' says the Lord of hosts, 'if I will not open for you the windows of heaven and pour out for you such blessing that there will not be room enough to receive it.'" The New Testament likewise abounds with tremendous monetary promises, such as Paul's words to the Corinthian church about financial giving. He affirms, "whoever sows bountifully will also reap bountifully" (II Corinthians 9:6).

I know that much, if not most, of what the Bible has to say about money comes by way of warning. Money can represent destruction and danger because it can arouse sin and dark passion in people. From Genesis to Revelation, we see that corruption, pride, indulgence, indifference to the poor, selfishness, and greed often stem from a love of money or a trust in riches.

As a pastor, I discovered that most believers have received very little training about handling finances. Even so, some of God's promises about income seemed so clear to me that a Christian would almost need help to misunderstand them! Yet, what the Bible said was possible didn't seem to be happening in the lives of many believers. I became convinced that to enjoy Biblical increase required education in what the Word of God says about money matters.

I knew practical answers had to exist somewhere. As I continued my search, both on behalf of the congregation I served and my own family, a light began to dawn in my heart. The Spirit of God revealed some insights that started to transform my own life financially. I started including some of these principles in my Sunday-morning teaching. I soon learned of their impact on those who heard. I realized that these messages had the potential to improve the course of a person's financial life. I also came to understand that God was using me to help others, some of whom were being energized to hit a financial home run both personally and in their businesses.

These events led to a more intense season of prayer. Through this time of intercession, the Lord impressed on me a vision in which I saw someone else as the pastor of the church I was then serving. I also saw myself teaching in churches all across the country, engaging in a ministry of reeducating Christians about Biblically rooted financial principles. As a part of that vision, I am putting on paper the truths I found. They have changed my life and continue to do so today.

Over several years of subsequent field ministry, I have seen some phenomenal results in people's finances. It has been a privilege to share with the Body of Christ things God has made very real to me. Apparently the Holy Spirit has made them real to many other people as well because their finances have likewise turned around.

Why do I use the phrase *Biblical increase*? Why not more common terms like *prosperity, financial success*, or *wealth*? One of my goals in this book is to avoid the kind of flag words or labels that invite stereotyping. I do not want

19

to lose anyone on the journey. My passion has been to search God's Word for fresh manna. My search has focused on the Scriptures much more than in the study of material otherwise available. In my travels, the word *increase* is not negative for most people, except perhaps after a hearty dinner when they look at the scales! It is a term and concept taken from Scripture; that is why I use it so frequently throughout this book.

I know the things you will learn have the potential to alter the course of your life financially if you will put their truth into practice. God's Word never fails. God wants to multiply your financial supply in order that you might use His resources to further His Kingdom. As you act on these principles, eternity will be impacted by your faithfulness to God.

My prayer is that you too will enter the turnaround process described in these pages. As you put these ideas to work, please write me. I would love to learn what God did through you. You can reach me by writing me care of my publisher whose address is at the bottom of this page.[1] Or contact me through my publisher on Internet.[2]

The first principle of Foolproof Finances is turning toward God's flow of money. It lays the groundwork for helping you change your money stream so that money can flow to you powerfully rather than away from you. You can learn about it on the very next page. Pray, and then discover what God has in store for you.

---

[1] David Mallonee • c/o Kingdom, Inc.
P.O. Box 486 • Mansfield, PA 16933

[2] Kingdom's internet address is http://www.kingdominc.com/

Chapter 2

Why Money Flows to Some People & Away from Others

Water is a powerful force. Since the beginning of creation, God has used it to shape and reshape this planet. A small stream may seem to have little significance, but when it combines with other streams it becomes a raging river. Anything traveling with that water is virtually unstoppable.

In fact, the life of a river is found in its movement. It must keep traveling onward in order to stay alive. If its flow were to stop, the water could quickly become stagnant and poisoned.

If you waded into a powerful river right now, one of the first things you would notice is the current. It forces you to adjust your footing and balance. It quickly shows you the direction the water is coming from. You can readily sense where the water is heading next. Obviously, your perspective will be noticeably different, depending on whether you are facing upstream or downstream.

This simple illustration makes a strong point about a Christian's finances. We may at times stand in the stream of the world's wealth and watch it flow powerfully away from us. At other times we may see that same wealth flowing toward us. The difference is one of perspective. Most people show keen interest in learning how to turn around so they can face the flow, allowing it to come their way.

Mark 4:25 contains one of Jesus' profound statements, one that eventually led me to the river analogy you have just read. Jesus said, "For whoever has, to him more will be given; but whoever does not have, even what he has will be taken away from him." Illumination of this teaching of Jesus is the first element that began turning me around financially.

In its most basic terms I understand this Bible verse to mean "the person who has something will get more, and the person who lacks will lose the little he or she already has."

That perspective runs contrary to how most people think. For example, if you assigned the average person to rewrite this section of the Bible, the results might read something like this: "The person who has something shouldn't get any more because he already has enough. The person who doesn't have anything should get something because, as the Lord knows, he needs it." This revised approach sounds like a deal that everyone would like!

We might wish Jesus had not said things the way He did, but the Word of God seems clear. Jesus observed that the person who has something will get more of what he already has; and the person who does not have anything will lose even the little he may have. This perspective is foundational Kingdom truth.

Not an Isolated Idea

Lest we misunderstand, two of the other Gospel accounts repeat this teaching—Matthew 13:12 and Luke 8:18. Jesus presents similar hard choices elsewhere as well. For instance, Luke 20:18 likens Christ to the chief cornerstone the builders rejected. If fallen humanity represents those builders, then we have only two alternatives. We can fall on the rock and be broken. Or the rock will fall on us and grind us to powder.

The direct context of Mark 4:25 deals with knowledge about the kingdom of heaven. But in it I hear a powerful truth that can apply to finances. Jesus' disciples seemed confused by His parables and asked why He communicated in this way. His reply? "To you it has been given to know the mystery of the kingdom of God; but to those who are outside, all things come in parables" (Mark 4:11). His followers are to "take heed what you hear; the measure you give will be the measure you get, and still more will be given to you" (Mark 4:24). Why? "For whoever has, to him more will be given; but whoever does not have, even what he has will be taken away from him" (Mark 4:25).

The human mind would like to look at this last verse and say, "It's simply not fair." If I stay in that mindset and refuse to fall on the rock, so to speak, then the rock will instead fall on me and grind me to powder. However, I can look at this verse and say, "This is Kingdom truth. It will never be altered. Therefore, I am going to willingly fall on this rock and let myself be broken in a godly way. I will let God change me and remake me. Then I am eligible to receive His blessings."

"It's that Verse Again"

I have given considerable thought to what Jesus said and how it applies spiritually. This caused me to recall the different seminars and meetings we had at the church building. I noticed with amazement that regardless of the topic or subject, usually the people who needed those special meetings the most were absent.

One time someone came in to teach on prayer. We had folks who complained about unanswered prayer: "I don't know why I cannot get answers" or "God doesn't seem to hear me when I pray." Does it not make sense that this kind of person would look at his or her calendar, reschedule any conflicting appointments, and make sure to be at the seminar? However, as I would look over the congregation, the people who grumbled the most about unanswered prayer were usually not there.

Guess who did attend the meetings on prayer? People who already prayed, received answers, and wanted to learn how to find more of God's heart. Initially, this reality frustrated me. When I understood Mark 4:25 and similar verses, I could look at the situation and say, "You know, it's that verse, 'to whoever has, more will be given.'"

I will never forget one situation as long as I live. Several folks in the church were having a difficult time locating and retaining a job. The church's leadership tried to help them. We prayed for them. I sent them different places where I thought they might be able to find employment. Then one of our leaders had a creative idea. "Pastor," he said, "why don't we have a job seminar for these folks? We can teach people how to dress for an interview. Let's also teach them how to fill out a job application correctly. We can ask people to bring their word processors and get everyone's résumé typed, and copies can be made. They can even go through simulated interviews in order to be mentally, emotionally, and spiritually prepared to find a job. Let's do everything we can to prepare them."

I considered this an excellent idea. We prepared spiritually by prayer and naturally by planning. We expected God to give great breakthroughs. We had our fellow members' interests at heart.

We gave personal invitations to some of those especially in need of a job. We pleaded with them to come. We tried to remove every obstacle by providing lunch, childcare, and even transportation. We were not having a job seminar because we needed something to do on a Saturday; our intent was to meet a very specific need for a number of individuals.

Because of God's faithfulness, the numerical response was good and the meeting was a success. I noted who attended with surprise. Hardly any of those who needed help attended. Instead, those who came to the job seminar were people who already had jobs. They wanted to learn how to get a better one. All I could say was, "It's that verse—Mark 4:25." "For whoever has, to him more will be given..."

Moving with God's Current

The Holy Spirit planted Mark 4:25 in my heart as a verse that pertains to finances in general and to my finances in particular. It taught me that I am either in a position where money flows *to* me or I am in a position where money flows *from* me.

What makes me think this verse applies to finances? Mark 4:25 is a general statement. Jesus states a life principle that seems to apply to every realm of life—spiritual, mental, emotional, physical, and financial. He did not say, "except in the realm of finances." Because He did not exclude money I believe it is appropriate to explore its implications for money as well.

I take the same approach with other general verses. For example, Luke 6:38 reads: "Give, and it will be given to you: good measure, pressed down, shaken together, and running over will be put into your bosom." This statement appears to be a kingdom-life principle. Obviously, Jesus is referring to many applications other than monetary ones. However, if Jesus did not mean these words to apply to income as well, then would He not have said, "except for finances."?

In Galatians 6:7-8, Paul echoes the same theme: "Whatsoever a man sows, that also will he reap." I assume "whatsoever" includes financial giving as well. Paul even makes a direct connection between giving and sowing in II Corinthians 9.

III John 2 says, "Beloved, I wish above all things that you prosper and be in health." Strong's *Concordance* interprets *prosper* as meaning to succeed in business affairs. The verse's context is that of a greeting. It links worldly well-being with the progress of the believer's soul.

Bible teachers from conservative to radical agree that nothing prohibits a Christian from trying to improve his or her financial condition. Of course, no Biblical values should be violated in the process. I believe God wants to have dominion over all areas of my life. Therefore, I eagerly look for verses that show me God's way, including financial matters.

Anyone Can Turn Around

This "flow" concept made me realize that even though I was a pastor and making a reasonably good salary, money was generally flowing *from* me. My financial net worth was negative with no turnaround in sight.

At that point, these realizations started to excite me. I had little enthusiasm for the idea that money was flowing *from* me. Rather, I had discovered that both sides of this verse are equally powerful. The stream can flow away from me, but if I can turn around, it can flow *to* me with equal force.

I was experiencing the wrong side of the verse, probably through my own mistakes or maybe through lack of training. In addition, I had been there for a long time. On faith, I praised God that He could make the changes needed to put me on the right side of the Mark 4:25 principle.

A river of water flows in one direction. I can face either downstream or upstream. If I want water to come to me, I do not have to change the direction of the current. Rather, the turn must occur in me as I face a new way.

I cannot alter the principle of Mark 4:25. I cannot deny the fact that Jesus said, "For whoever has, to him more will be given." What I can do, however, is allow the Holy Spirit to direct and inspire changes in me. God's work can turn me around and position me on the right side of this verse.

Dealing with the Holes

Dollar amounts are irrelevant. The truth of Mark 4:25 has absolutely nothing to do with how much money a person makes. Rather, its application involves a spiritual principle, such as what the prophet Haggai outlines:

Now this is what the Lord Almighty says: "Give careful thought to your ways. You have planted much, but have harvested little. You eat, but never have enough. You drink, but never have your fill. You put on clothes, but are not warm. You earn wages, only to put them in a purse with holes in it" (Haggai 1:5-6 NIV).

The wallets and pocketbooks of today were called money bags in Haggai's time. When Christians ask for God's financial blessing, our focus is typically on God pouring more in the top. "If I just had $150 more a month, everything would be so much better," someone says. "Come on, Lord, please pour more in," another prays.

What if God looked in our money bag and all He saw was daylight? Suppose something had blown a huge hole in the bottom of the pouch. Would it make sense for Him to keep shoveling more in the top?

If God pours $10,000 a year into a "holey" money bag, how much will be left? Nothing. If you could convince God to pour in ten times as much—for a total of $100,000—how much will be left? Still nothing! What if God poured in a hundred times that original amount—$1,000,000—how much would remain? The same as if He had given you nothing! My point is that financial increase has little to do with how much money goes in the top. Greater amounts of cash flow might generate more fun. But your net residue would still basically be the same.

I have had occasion to counsel with individuals who earn relatively high incomes. In spite of this substantial cash flow, they were having financial difficulty. The remarks they made were familiar: "I don't know where it all went"; "I don't have much to show for it"; etc. They often had a debt problem as well. Such stories illustrate that money can flow from us, even if the income is large. If I have a "hole" in my money bag and God increases the amount of money He pours in, then all I might end up with is complications on an even bigger scale than before.

The Holy Spirit's work is to focus us on the bottom of the bag. I believe the wisdom of God tells the believer to find out what created the hole. The next step is to find out what is necessary to repair it. In plain English, the Holy Spirit can help you discover that God has already been providing better than you thought He was. Second, you will discover that it is easier to ask God to pour more into the top when you know in your heart that you have repaired the hole in the bottom.

Habits and Actions that Lead to Holes

Before we can turn around financially, we need to learn what creates the money flow away from us. Haggai likens this flow to a hole in the bottom of a money bag. As I sought the Lord on why money flows either powerfully from us or to us, He led me to examine two distinct themes of my life.

The first area that stood out is what I call "Habits and Actions." I call the second group "Attitudes and Motives." My response to these two groups puts me in a position either of money flowing *to* me powerfully or of money flowing *from* me powerfully.

The Book of Proverbs provides great help. It often speaks of normal, human impulses that are not wrong in and of themselves. Proverbs shows that these impulses, when allowed to go out of control, become offensive habits and actions that squander the provision God has already made. They hammer at us until we reach a place of lack.

Solomon was the richest man of his day, and was also considered the wisest. Some of his wisdom is taught in the Proverbs including his knowledge about accumulating, investing, and protecting the provisions God had given him. Woven throughout the Proverbs are some 20 to 25 verses that show cause-and-effect relationships about income: "If you do this, you will lose money" or "if this action repeats itself in your life, money will go from you to a stranger" or "If such-and-such an impulse is out of control in your life, it will head you in the direction of poverty."

The Proverbs are not speaking of what someone does to reach heaven after death. The habits and actions addressed have little, if anything, to do with whether our sins have been forgiven. I have no doubt you can show up at heaven's pearly gates with your checkbook unbalanced, your credit cards way over their limits, and your life in terrible financial straits. If you have been washed in the blood of Jesus Christ, God will still welcome you in.

Rather, Proverbs focuses on how tough it can be between here and the pearly gates. Out-of-control impulses make it unlikely God will bring larger amounts of resources into the believer's life. Taking external dominion first requires taking internal dominion.

In my study of Proverbs, I have identified three basic categories. I describe the first as *spiritual and moral actions*. Proverbs is very clear here. If someone becomes immoral or perverse in his or her lifestyle, such as by engaging in adultery or fornication, the text says very clearly that, "strangers [will] obtain your wealth" (Proverbs 5:10 TLB). Immorality and perverseness in lifestyle open a door that leads to both spiritual and financial consequences.

The wisdom of Solomon also adds that if I'm rebellious, if I do not heed good counsel, if I cover my sins, then I will not prosper. These are all spiritual and moral actions.

I see a second category of Proverbs. I call them *financial mistakes*. This is the area where I was personally suffering the most. Solomon's wisdom covers virtually all the possible financial mistakes a person can make. They speak of those who are not generous with the Lord or with others. They also discuss the unwise use of debt in which "the borrower is servant to the lender" (Proverbs 22:7 NIV). Arguably, not all debt is created equal. The most crushing is the uncollateralized kind that brings in no income and ends up on credit cards. I was reminded that paying 15 to 20 percent interest is like having a siphon hose in my back pocket. I resolved to stop accumulating this kind of debt immediately, if not sooner.

Proverbs indicates the need for having a simple, easy-to-use budget. "Any enterprise is built by wise planning, becomes strong through common sense, and profits wonderfully by keeping abreast of the facts" (Proverbs 24:3-4 TLB). Christians need to study about money management for believers. We must learn to budget as well as make wise purchases. These are two of the wisest things you could ever do financially. As the adage goes, "When my outgo exceeds my income, then my upkeep becomes my downfall." I decided it was personally necessary to bring more of my spending under control.

The third category of these Proverbs involves *work habits*. I learn that if I am not diligent in my work habits, if I am not consistent, faithful, steady, and reliable, then poverty will come upon me (see Proverbs 10:4). These Scriptures give a graphic illustration of the power of poverty: it will come upon me like an armed man (see Proverbs 24:30-34). Even generous giving cannot compensate for laziness or lack of diligence. Industry and faithfulness are necessary ingredients to God's overall financial plan.

God's Word is not saying that if I make a mistake, I will be in irreparable trouble. He is addressing the result of impulses that are out of control. These habits and actions can become patterns that in turn become lifestyles and gradually become strongholds. Some strongholds are an extension of ones from previous generations. They do not take dominion overnight. They can, however, lock out money.

First Things First

I find a pattern in the Scriptures that God usually deals with character flaws before He prospers a person.

> *"I traverse the way of righteousness, in the midst of the paths of justice, that I may cause those who love me to inherit wealth, that I may fill their treasuries"* (Proverbs 8:20-21, emphasis added.)

The King James Version reads, "In the midst of the paths of *judgment*" (Proverbs 8:20b, emphasis added). The same idea appears in the New Testament where we are called to judge ourselves (see I Corinthians 11:31-32). According to these and other verses, the wisdom of God will lead us to the point where we examine ourselves. We may also experience godly sorrow that leads to repentance (II Corinthians 7:10). Self-judgment seems to be a prerequisite for receiving God's full inheritance, including material blessing.

We should desire the Heavenly Father to purge our character flaws before we experience increase. It is critical as we turn into the stream and money begins flowing toward us. Your financial stream may be a trickle now, but as you apply some of the things written in this book, it can and will become a rushing river. You will want your feet solidly planted on "the Rock" to prevent being swept away.

In summary, the Book of Proverbs identifies many specific habits and/or actions that bring financial loss, including those listed below:

Habits and Actions to Avoid
(All verses taken from Proverbs unless otherwise noted.)

Spiritual and Moral Actions

Covering sins (Proverbs 28:13 KJV) "He...shall not prosper...."

Ignoring the poor (21:13 KJV) "...he also shall cry himself, but shall not be heard."

Immorality (5:10 KJV) "Lest strangers be filled with thy wealth..." (see also 29:3).

Getting money by wickedness (10:3 KJV) "The Lord...casteth away the substance of the wicked."

Keeping vain companions (28:19 KJV) "...shall have poverty enough."

Loving pleasure or wine (21:17 KJV) "He...shall be a poor man...."

Overeating (23:21 KJV) ...shall come to poverty...."

Refusing correction (13:18 KJV) "Poverty and shame shall be to [you]...."

Troubling your family (11:29 KJV) "...shall inherit the wind...."

(Other Bible students have found additional harmful actions)[1]

Financial Mistakes

Co-signing a note (11:15 KJV) "He that is surety for a stranger shall smart for it...."

Not being generous with the Lord and others (11:24 KJV) "...it tendeth to poverty" (see also Malachi 3:10-11).

Getting money without labor (13:11 KJV) "...shall be diminished...."

Unwise use of credit (22:7) Note: An incentive to being debt-free is to think about what could be done (both giving and increasing) with that money if it wasn't servicing all that debt.

Giving to the rich (22:16 KJV) "...shall surely come to want."

Charging usury (28:8 KJV) "...he shall gather it for him that will pity the poor."

Get-rich-quick schemes (28:22 KJV) "...poverty shall come upon him" (see also 20:21; 21:5).

Lack of sales resistance (14:15 KJV) "The simple believeth every word...."

---

[1] Neglecting the House of God (Haggai 1) and Not trusting the man of God (II Chronicles 20:20). See *War on Debt* by Dr. John Avanzini. (Fort Worth, Tex.: HIS Publishing, 1991), p. 106.

Not having a budget (24:3-4 TLB) "Any enterprise is built by wise planning...."

Work Habits

Sleeping too much (6:11 KJV) "So shall thy poverty come...."

Not being diligent (10:4 KJV) "He becometh poor...."

Talking too much (14:23 NAS) "...leads only to poverty."

Slothfulness (19:15 KJV) "...shall suffer hunger."

Chasing fantasies (28:19 NIV) "...will have his fill of poverty."[2]

Holes Caused by Attitudes and Motives

The Book of James was written to Christians who desired material things. They had been asking God for them but were not receiving. James addresses the cause: they were extreme in their greed. We may not be consumed with greed as they were, but there still could be room for the Holy Spirit to do some adjustment in our lives.

You ask and do not receive, because you ask amiss, that you may spend it on your pleasures (James 4:3).

---

[2] Some of this material on the Proverbs was drawn from Bill Gothard's *Men's Manual*, Volume II, Revised Edition, June 1984, 3rd Printing. (Oak Brook, Ill.: Institute in Basic Life Principles).

I like this verse in the New American Standard. It says, "You ask and do not receive, because you ask with *wrong motives...* (emphasis added)." The passage teaches me that right motives lead to receiving. It is refreshing to learn that God thinks I can have a few nice things, such as perhaps a better car, house, or choice of clothes, and He will not be angry at me.

The Bible teaches that Christians can experience increase. However, with a little human greed mixed in, that pure Bible message becomes a strange concoction. Greed can twist someone's outlook so the true desire of the heart is this: "I am so thankful for the Bible message on increase because God knows I love stuff. God knows I want a new house and a new car. I cannot wait to have more money in the bank." God must do such a work in our heart that we genuinely want the Kingdom of God to be advanced. At the same time we can recognize that God does not object if our standard of living goes up in the process.

The Bible abounds with the negative aspects of attitudes and motives. Even non-Christians are aware of Paul's admonition to Timothy that "the love of money is a root of all kinds of evil" (I Timothy 6:10 NIV).

Another widely known truth is what Jesus told His disciples in Matthew 6:24, "You cannot serve God and mammon." Jesus was addressing motives. Unfortunately, thinking along faulty lines takes a verse like "You cannot serve God and money" and adds an explanation to it such as, "because God doesn't want you to have any." Jesus' point, I believe, in no way excludes His followers from having money. Rather, He was warning against making decisions in life based on what it means for our pocketbooks, what it will cost us financially, or what it will not cost us. When our values are money driven, the day will come when the spirit behind mammon will turn on us and absolutely devour us.

On the other hand, if I make my decisions based on what the will of God is for my life, the principles of God, or how the Bible speaks to a situation, then I have pure motives. If I make my decisions based on the principles of God regardless of what appears to be the monetary cost, then the spirit behind the mammon cannot tear me down. Pure motives become my spiritual protection. I am then better positioned to handle more of His resources.

The Upside to Attitudes and Motives

The New Testament teaching about finances is a fine blend of warnings and promises. I must not neglect one or the other. I desire to heed the warnings and believe the promises. I must be sensitive to both sides of the equation.

Proverbs 22:4 reads, "By humility and the fear of the Lord are riches and honor and life." Humility is an attitude; the fear of the Lord is a motive. So this verse implies that if the right attitudes and motives find a place in my heart, then instead of riches, honor, and life flowing *from* me, they can flow *to* me.

I can quickly evaluate my motives by measuring them against Matthew 6:33:

But seek first the kingdom of God and His righteousness, and all these things shall be added to you (Matthew 6:33).

"Seek first the Kingdom of God" means having God's interests at heart. Whatever is important to Him must be important to us. If I have His interests at heart, "all these things," including financial provision, will then be added to me. My standard of living is positively affected by what is "added"!

Job's Drastic Turnaround

There are instances in the Scriptures where Bible characters experienced drastic turnarounds in their finances. First, money would flow to them powerfully. Then change occurred for various reasons and money would begin flowing from them. In the midst of their struggle, they would have an experience with God. He would speak a word of such magnitude it brought internal change. The change turned them around on the inside. Then they returned to the original position of money flowing to them powerfully.

Job provides an excellent example. As the book that bears his name begins, Job had money flowing to him powerfully. He was not merely a rich man; he was the richest man in the East. When money began flowing away from him, virtually overnight Job went from being the richest man in the East to one of the poorest. For approximately nine months, Job languished in this situation. He became angry with the Lord, chiding God for treating him unjustly (Job 9:28-35) and cursing the day of his birth (Job 3). Job relied on his own righteousness to sustain him, (see Job 27:6) instead of putting his trust in God. These attitudes and actions are not in accord with living in right relationship with God, and became a stronghold in Job. His friends offered their help. "Job, you've done this," they said. Or,

"Job, you've done that." They presented explanations based on human understanding.

Men did not have the answer for Job. The story does not end there, however. Job 38:1 says, "Then the Lord answered Job out of the whirlwind...." God spoke to Job. First He said, in essence, "Job, go take a bath, put on some clean clothes, and then come back and answer Me like a man." Those words seem to be strong words for a man who has just lost everything. He was hurting and had boils on his body. Yet when Job returned, the Lord continued, "Were you around when I made this?", "Were you there when I created that?", and "Were you present when the angels did thus and so?"

Job had fallen into a stronghold: he was held by the power of his own anger and self-righteousness. He was locked in and the money was locked out. Those strong words from God were attacking the stronghold in Job. I know it was difficult for Job to hear them, but those words were pulling apart that stronghold. Weak words will not break strongholds; it takes strong words to break them. God was telling Job the truth.

Christians sometimes think that if we had only a little more money every month, our finances would be better. Yet we actually need something more than additional money. We need God to tell us the truth. God told Job the truth and the stronghold was ripped into pieces. In Job 42:6 Job repents, which means to turn around. He changed on the inside. Job was set free. Then Job 42:10 says, "And the Lord restored Job's losses when he prayed for his friends. Indeed the Lord gave Job twice as much as he had before."

Job had turned around in life by first turning around inside. One outcome was money again flowing to him as powerfully, or even more powerfully, than it had earlier. Job would probably have been happy if God had made him just as rich as he was before. But God made him twice as rich! Now consider Job 42:11:

Then all his brothers, all his sisters, and all those who had been his acquaintances before, came to him and ate food with him in his house; and they consoled him and comforted him for all the adversity that the Lord had brought upon him. Each one gave him a piece of silver and each a ring of gold.

Where were these folks three months ago when Job really needed them? A little money and a little gold would certainly have been nice six months earlier. When Job lost everything he had and was broke, no one brought him money or gold. Now God makes him twice as rich as before, and then friends come bringing money and gold. Job's experience illustrates the verse emphasized at the beginning of this chapter, Mark 4:25: "For whoever has, to him more will be given; but whoever does not have, even what he has will be taken away from him."

I believe Job's friends did not offer him money and gold earlier because his stronghold had them locked out. Now that the stronghold had been torn down, God could bless him and make him twice as rich as he was before. His friends were also free to bring money and gold.

The turning point for Job started with a word from God. It changed him on the inside. Job shifted to the positive side of the principle in Mark 4:25.

Joseph Also Turned into the Flow

Certain events in Joseph's life also help us understand how to turn into God's flow. Psalm 105:16-18 reads, "Moreover He called for a famine in the land; He destroyed all the provision of bread. He sent a man before them— Joseph—who was sold as a slave. They hurt his feet with fetters, he was laid in irons." Joseph was sent to Egypt by his brothers and sold as a slave. Later he was thrown into prison for a crime he did not commit. Joseph found himself in a literal, physical, earthly prison. A Hebrew in an Egyptian prison would feel totally hopeless. Joseph was locked into a future that seemed to have no way out.

We can liken Joseph's physical prison to the financial prison we can find ourselves in. It requires only a mistake here, an accident there, a lack of knowledge over here, and before we know it, we are locked in. Maybe we have hit the peak of our earning potential and we are trapped between that limit and the rising cost of living. Perhaps we are also affected by the financial mistakes we have made. Our financial situation can be a prison just as real as Joseph's, can it not?

Joseph's story would be a sad one if not for the next word. That word contains much hope. Psalm 105:18-19 continues, "He was laid in irons **until** the time that his word came to pass...." The King James Version says, "Until the time that his word *came* (emphasis added)." A word came from God that set Joseph free. It broke him out of that prison and freed him from his shackles. In addition it opened up whole new horizons. It made things possible that would have been impossible before.

If I am in a financial prison, I need the same experience. I need a word from God of such magnitude and power that it sets me free from prison and opens up whole new horizons. Things previously impossible will become possible.

This word did more than set Joseph free. Verse 19 continues, "...The word of the Lord tested him." The word translated *tested* also means "to refine or purify." God's word to Joseph not only set him free, it also purified and refined him. It made this human vessel of higher quality. It made him more useful. God had plans for Joseph that included being the prime minister of Egypt. When his brothers came to buy grain during the famine, Joseph could have taken revenge. But the word had so purified him that he refused to retaliate. Granted, he did have a little fun with them first by testing their sincerity (see Genesis 42—44).

When Joseph revealed himself to his brothers, he made a statement that sounds as if it belongs in the New Testament. It speaks volumes. According to Genesis 45:7, he said, "And God sent me...to save your lives by a great deliverance." Joseph brought life, he brought deliverance, and he cared for his brothers. Are not these actions precisely what the New Testament Church is supposed to do?

In Egypt Joseph experienced one of the largest wealth transfers that had ever taken place on the face of planet Earth. The Scriptures below reveal the magnitude.

Joseph collected all the money that was to be found in Egypt and Canaan in payment for the grain they were buying, and he brought it to Pharaoh's palace. When the money of the people of Egypt and Canaan was gone, all Egypt came to Joseph and said, "Give us food. Why should we die before your eyes? Our money is used up." "Then bring your livestock," said Joseph. "I will sell you food in exchange for your livestock, since your money is gone." So they brought their livestock to Joseph, and he gave them food in exchange for their horses, their sheep and goats, their cattle and donkeys.... They came to him the following year and said, "We cannot hide from our lord the fact that since our money is gone and our livestock belongs to you, there is nothing left for our lord except our bodies and our land. Why should we perish before your eyes—we and our land as well? Buy us and our land in exchange for food"... So Joseph bought all the land in Egypt for Pharaoh... because the famine was too severe for them. The land became Pharaoh's (Genesis 47:14-20 NIV).

The typical person receiving that much wealth would tend to forget God's overall purposes. The temptations of mammon might be too overwhelming. But the word to Joseph had set him free; it had purified him and burned God's overall purpose into his heart. He remembered God's purpose was to bring life, deliverance, and care for his brothers.

God could trust Joseph with that much money. Joseph had been so purified that he would release the money to bring life, deliverance, and care for his brothers. What about Joseph's standard of living? Since his motives were pure and he was willing to release the money to bring life, his standard of living improved along the way. He enjoyed the best of Egypt. He lived in a palace instead of a prison; he wore Pharaoh's ring and rode in the second chariot of Pharaoh (see Genesis 41:42-43).

In Conclusion

Matthew 6:33 presents a balance. Seeking first the Kingdom of God addresses my *motives*; it calls my motives to the highest possible level. Seeking His righteousness brings His character into my *habits* and *actions*; I am to permit His righteousness to come from the inside to the outside. Doing so can not only make me prosper spiritually, but also financially. As transformations occur in my motives, habits and actions, I become a better steward of the resources God entrusts to me. This enables me to safely experience an improved standard of living.

Certain attitudes and motives can disqualify us from handling God's resources on a larger scale. Undisciplined impulses can diminish the provision God has already made. Each one of us needs a Joseph experience. We can look to the Lord for a word in due season. We can look for a word of that same forcefulness that will start breaking us out, ripping apart strongholds and opening up new horizons.

The net effect will be a burning away of unscriptural attitudes and motives. The purposes of God will be sealed in our heart and we will experience an increased desire to release provision for those purposes. The wisdom of God could lead us through the necessary paths of judgment. These preparations are vital if God is to fill our treasuries.

In Job's life and Joseph's life, a direct word from God was the turning point. We must be willing to let God tell us the truth. He will, in His own loving way. In response, each believer must decide what he or she wants more: the stronghold or to know and live the truth?

Questions

1. What has God said to you through this chapter about your finances?

2. How might God use upcoming experiences to purify your motives?

3. What changes need to be made in your life to put you on the right side of Mark 4:25?

4. For what purposes of God will you release money in the future?

Key Action Points:

I. Identify the holes:
> What habits and actions cause you to surrender
>   money to the world's system?
> What motives render you incapable of handling
>   resources on a larger scale?

II. Determine to Change:
> Habits and Actions
> Attitudes and Motives

III. Ask the Lord to purify and refine you
IV. Listen to the Lord
V. Spend time reading the book of Proverbs

Chapter 3

Three Keys to Turning Around

Are you interested in building a solid financial future? I believe God has that desire for you. He wants you to take dominion over the state of your finances. He wants you to have an adequate and bountiful supply. Part of this process of gaining dominion over your future finances involves how you perceive yourself. Do you view yourself as a steward of another's resources? Or do you believe you have personal ownership over what is in your care?

The answer to those questions appears to be the primary truth about finances throughout the Scriptures. If you do not understand this truth, then what the Bible says about finances will never fit together properly.

10 Percent or 100 Percent?

Scripturally speaking, God is the owner and I am the steward. This idea is repeated throughout the Scriptures, beginning in the very first chapter of the very first book

47

(see Genesis 1:26-28). Psalm 24:1 reads, "The earth is the Lord's, and all its fullness, the world and those who dwell therein." Another Scripture confirms this truth: "'The silver is Mine, and the gold is Mine,' says the Lord of hosts" (Haggai 2:8). The earth, its resources, its property, its silver and gold, and other tangible assets—100 percent—belong to the Lord.

If God is in the position of ownership, then we are stewards. Our job is to manage His resources. After all, by definition a steward manages the resources and the estate of another individual. He uses the assets in ways which benefit the owner. Since God has declared His ownership of all my material and monetary items, my function is to manage the resources He guides into my life. By contrast the philosophy of this world states, "I am the owner." As a Christian, I should recognize that statement as error.

However, a certain line of thought filters into many churches with enough of a spiritual sound to remain undetected as error. It says, "10 percent is God's and 90 percent is mine." Yet that statement is not Biblically correct. Rather, 100 percent is God's. He is the owner and I have the glorious position of being the manager: the steward of a portion of those assets.

Whenever I mention stewardship and say God is the owner, some people become nervous. In their minds, they may be thinking, *If God is the owner, He probably wants me to give it all away.* However, the above truth does not require the believer to give everything away on an "every dime every time" basis.

A steward is expected to manage resources according to the will of Him who owns it, not according to his own will. Such is the steward's safety; it is also his or her reward. In light of my stewardship of God's resources, I manage the portion He puts in my life according to His will and not according to my will. That solid foundation is how we exercise financial dominion over the future.

Your Never-Miss Financial Advisor

We live in unstable times. This uncertainty is a part of our fallen realm; the Bible speaks of things that can and cannot be shaken (see Hebrews 12:26-27). Such shaking would predictably include the world's economic system and its financial markets. How will we face such a future? Will it be in our own strength and wisdom, or as stewards of the Most High, moving in the mind of Christ? Put that way, is there really a choice for the disciple of Jesus?

I do not know what tomorrow holds. However, as I enter the future, God is coming out of it. He has already been there. He is uniquely positioned to advise me about my finances today, based on what He knows will happen ahead. Therefore, every leading He gives me today about different aspects of my money and stewardship is not necessarily for His benefit alone, but for mine as well. He can instruct me to do something today to prepare for what He knows will happen in the future.

The Lord can see events a year from now, call us by name and say, "I want you to do this today." I take His instruction by faith, knowing that He is preparing me for the future. The instruction may be about giving; it may be help with money management; or it may be about an investment I should make.

Even the best human financial advisor cannot be certain of what will happen tomorrow, much less next month or year. Believers, on the other hand, have an advisor who "...will tell you things to come" (John 16:13). I believe the Holy Spirit's advice even extends into the realm of personal finances. God's communication comes both in the form of general principles from the Word as well as specific instructions from His voice in my heart.

Overlooked Dimensions of Stewardship

Stewardship has three aspects. I find stewards in the parables of Jesus functioning in all three of these capacities. Many church people have heard far more about one of these aspects than about the other two.

The most widely discussed dimension is generally referred to as *giving*. It involves tithes, offerings, alms to the poor, missionary support, and other gifts to God's work. A second, lesser emphasized aspect is *managing*. A third aspect could be called *increasing*.

I believe God's intention is that I, as a steward, skillfully weave these three aspects together. As I do so, I build a solid financial future. It does not matter what happens in the economy or in the halls of government; my finances are secure. Someone has wisely said that what affects my personal finances are not so much decisions made at the White House as ones made at my house. No one can affect my finances any more than I can.

A Widespread Lie about Giving

From God's perspective, I will have a solid financial future only if I am a giver. Biblical increase begins here. Whether the issue is tithes, offerings, alms to the poor, or missionary gifts, the devil tries to hit a person with one of two different lies about giving.

Deception number one goes like this: "If you give that money to God, you'll never see it again." Wrong. I see at least two ways in which the money can be seen again, one eternal and one temporal. For instance, the angel told Cornelius in Acts 10:4, "Your prayers and your alms have come up for a memorial before God." Cornelius regularly gave money to feed the poor. His giving was as an everlasting memorial before God. Since God does not show favoritism, my giving also builds a memorial before God. I anticipate seeing the memorial that my giving built.

A second manner in which I can see the money I gave again is mentioned by Paul in Philippians 4:17: "Not that I seek the gift, but I seek the fruit that abounds to your account." The Philippians had more in their account because they *sent* an offering. This account couldn't have been their earthly one—the money had been given to Paul. Where was the account which had increased?

Jesus uses some very intriguing words in Matthew 6:19-20: "Do not lay up for yourselves treasures on earth... but lay up for yourselves treasures in heaven." Anyone knows how to store wealth on this earth. We can put funds into a savings account or buy more property.

Can we do the same in a literal way with treasures in heaven? Are treasures in heaven as real as treasures on earth? Without a doubt, they are equally real. This heavenly reserve or account is there when we need it. It is a divine mechanism which enables us to effectively deal with a hostile financial environment.

It is an amazing concept that I as a Christian have two accounts: earthly and heavenly. The earthly one often comes up short. Its insufficiency, however, does not mean I am broke. I can have a zero balance in my earthly account, but still have substantial resources in my heavenly one.

Sometimes a believer looks to his or her earthly account and finds it lacking. Then this Christian turns to the heavenly account and discovers nothing there either. At that point, the person is officially broke. Why? It's because this person has not been laying up treasure in heaven. Only a merciful divine bailout will rescue this person.

How is our heavenly account funded? Who or what creates these reserves? A primary answer is given by Jesus:

Sell what you have and give to those in need. This will fatten your purses in heaven! And the purses of heaven have no rips or holes in them (Luke 12:33a TLB).

Biblically directed giving builds up those heavenly treasures. The Philippians were discovering the wonder of this truth. If you have not been honoring the Lord with your gifts, I urge you to repent and begin giving to the Lord the finances He requests. You will strike a critical blow to financial bondage.

Remember, giving is not because God needs the money. No one in heaven needs the almighty dollar. Rather, I should give because I love God. My giving then becomes an investment that lasts. It is more secure than having gold bullion in a guarded vault.

The following example should help you visualize how the two accounts, earthly and heavenly, work together. Suppose, for instance, you were a wealthy individual in a country rife with hyperinflation, where the price of bread or gasoline doubled on a weekly basis. In order for your money not to lose its value, you would transfer a significant portion of it into the currency of a more stable nation. You would literally send it to another realm. This would cause your funds to last because a stable currency retains its value against a rapidly inflating one. Then when you needed buying power, you would exchange the money and whatever interest you had made back into the currency of your own nation. In the same way, money invested in your heavenly account does not lose its purchasing power. It becomes a hedge in changing economic environments.

In Matthew 6:19, Jesus said harmful things can happen to money stored in the earthly realm. It can be stolen or taxed. Unwise economic policies can affect our money. Some may say, "I don't need to transfer money to a heavenly account; America has a strong economy. After all, we have streets paved with asphalt." When compared to heaven, even the industrially strong United States is an underdeveloped, insolvent entity. Streets of gold are superior to streets of asphalt any day. Giving to God through tithes, offerings, alms, and missions allows believers to transfer some of our wealth into a heavenly currency—lay up treasures in heaven—where it cannot be touched by the action of men. Thieves such as inflation, deflation, and recession cannot break in and steal. Then, as needed, I can turn to my heavenly account and through prayer, faith, and hearing God's voice, draw from those ever-growing resources. As a result I again see the money I have given away.

What kind of return can I expect on these heavenly investments? Jesus spoke of a hundredfold return (Mark 10:29-30). This amount seems so unrealistic in our fallen world where an annual long-term gain of 12 to 14% is considered quite good. (As someone has said, what else can be expected in a society where our approach to curing inflation with deflation is equivalent to running over a man with a truck, then in order to apologize, backing over him!) What might happen to investments in a realm that always has growth, never has recession, and has policies that never need rewriting? An economist would tell you there is no way to calculate results in such a healthy environment. No one has a model to go by. Maybe that incredible growth is what Jesus meant by "hundredfold"?

Tell the rich people... to be happy to give and ready to share. By doing that they will be saving treasure for themselves in heaven: that treasure will be a strong foundation. Their future life can be built on that treasure... (I Timothy 6:18-19 NCV).

Make no mistake, those deposits via tithes, offerings, giving to the poor, and missionary support are vital. Two spectacular things happen when we make them. We gain the satisfaction of obeying God and of making funds available that help meet both spiritual and physical needs around us. At the same time, our heavenly reserves are increased. What a Kingdom!

A Second Lie from Satan

The father of lies (see John 8:44) sometimes hits believers with a second falsehood. He says, "If you keep giving that money to God, your standard of living will be a lot less than what it could be." Again, this is absolutely wrong. Consider Jesus' teaching in Luke 12:42: "And the Lord said, 'Who then is that faithful and wise steward, whom his master will make ruler over his household, to give them their portion of food in due season?'" A steward's responsibility, seen here, is to meet a need that we see to ensure that you receive your "portion of food" in due season. Believers have this responsibility one to another in the Body of Christ. The next verse, Luke 12:43, reads, "Blessed is that servant whom his master will find so doing when he comes." *Blessed* might mean only that the servant will feel good and have a warm, fuzzy glow in his heart. But verse 44 tells me specifically how he will be blessed: "Truly, I say to you that he will make him ruler over all that he has."

If God proportionately makes you and me rulers over all that He has, what would happen to our standard of living? Our standard of living would be forced to go up. As I, a steward, look out for other stewards, God will one day say, "I will make you ruler, proportionately, over all that I have." As He begins diverting more resources into my life, it is absolutely inevitable that my standard of living will start rising. After all, even words like *billions* and *trillions* do not begin to describe all the world's wealth.

Most people are more familiar with making deposits into our heavenly account than with making withdrawals. The latter parts of this book deal mostly with the withdrawal concept.

Managing Helps Money Go Farther

A second aspect of stewardship involves managing the money I spend to meet my needs. *Foolproof Finances* proposes that God does not mind if I spend a sizable portion of His money on myself and my family. However, when I spend His resources on myself, He wants me to get value for what I spend. A statement Jesus made following the feeding of the 5,000 brings insight into God's attitudes about waste. "Gather up the fragments that remain, so that nothing is lost" (John 6:12b). He is more than abundant; everyone there was filled. Then the extra was gathered and put to good use. Functional stewardship can be described as abundant, but not wasteful.

Managing involves at least three steps. First, I need to know how to make wise purchases and get value for God's money. For instance, if I plan to buy a house, good stewardship calls me to buy the most house for the least amount of money. Wisdom teaches me to look for a house that I can reasonably expect to appreciate in value in three to five years. (I can study this idea by using books from the local library.) The same principle applies if I am buying a car, or if I am going to spend hundreds of dollars a year on insurance. I should be an informed steward. This skill will help me weather the economic fluctuations of earthly life.

Second, I should learn how to live within a simple budget. The purpose is to insure that my outgo does not exceed my income. This is the only way to get out of debt and stay out.

Third, I must take care of the things I already have. For example, why would my Heavenly Father provide a nicer car if I trash or misuse the one I now drive?

I believe managing must come before increasing. As I mentioned in Chapter 2 from Haggai 1:6, repairing holes in the money bag is necessary before God's people can experience abundance. Good management limits the devil's access to our finances. Malachi 3:11 records God's promise to "... rebuke the devourer for your sakes, so that he will not destroy the fruit of your ground." Sometimes our lack of Biblical money management makes us a devourer. If so, we need the Father to reprove us.

We cannot avoid economic fluctuations in this life. God has promised to meet all our needs, including financial ones. However, many of us have been drowning in our own mistakes. God will deliver us, but not necessarily along a straight, arrow-like path. Our upward climb will probably be more like a series of higher highs followed by higher lows. Some economic fluctuations happen personally, some regionally, and some are national or international. However, if I have learned God's values toward money, and how to handle it according to Biblical precepts, then that knowledge will help steer me through those economic fluctuations.

Increasing Is the Final Fruit

A third aspect of stewardship is "increasing." This dynamic involves a modest portion of the money that comes into our lives. The goal is to invest it for future returns.

Stewards in the parables of Jesus demonstrated this function of stewardship. (We will examine several of those parables later in this book.)

In one of many Old Testament verses about increasing, Isaiah 48:17 states, "Thus says the Lord, your Redeemer, the Holy One of Israel: 'I am the Lord your God, who teaches you to profit, who leads you by the way you should go.'" I am intrigued by the phrase, "teaches you to profit." Why does the Lord have to teach us about it? Profit does not come naturally to the fallen human condition. Beginning with the patriarchs, God imparted information to His covenant people that became a part of their heritage. Those lessons are sprinkled throughout the Old and New Testaments. Unfortunately, there is no one place where they are listed step by step. Possibly there were certain concepts that both the writers and the readers of Scripture understood and did not need explanation. For us, it will take the illumination of the Holy Spirit to synthesize these ideas.

The remainder of this book is primarily devoted to pulling together those lessons. Increase is an exciting subject that can benefit anyone, regardless of background, who is a serious follower of the Lord Jesus Christ.

In Summary

Can you see, as we weave together these three dimensions of stewardship, how we are building a financial future that neither hell nor the systems of this world can shake? Each aspect is important in its own right. Excess in one will not compensate for lack in another. For instance, generous giving will not overcome gross mismanagement or poor work habits. These three work hand in hand, just as "...a threefold cord is not quickly broken" (Ecclesiastes 4:12b).

Giving, managing, and increasing are all balanced in the mind of God. As He entrusts His resources to me, I believe I should return a portion to Him in the form of tithes and offerings. Another substantial portion will be spent on meeting the needs of my family, which may include raising our standard of living. The other portion should be set aside for investment for a future return. I need to be sensitive in order to know how much should be given, how much should be spent on the family, and how much I should set aside for the purpose of increasing. The mix will probably vary according to the different seasons of my life. You as a steward unto God must discern the proper ratio for the various seasons of your life.

Questions

1. What makes you confident that your heavenly account is properly funded?

2. Based on this chapter, what changes will you make in how you spend God's money?

3. Do you presently set aside money each month for the purpose of increasing? Why or why not?

Key Action Points:

I. Recognize yourself as a steward
II. Evaluate what the Lord would have you to do in each of the three aspects of stewardship:

1. Giving
   What has God laid on my heart to give?
2. Managing
   What can I do to make wiser purchases and get better value from the money I'm spending?
   What changes do I need to implement so I can learn to live on a budget?
   How can I take better care of what I already own?
3. Increasing
   How would the Lord have me to multiply the resources he has already entrusted to me?

Chapter 4

How Bible Characters Multiplied Money

I was kneeling one Tuesday morning beside the church altar asking the Lord what I should teach on the upcoming Sunday. While listening for God's leading, I realized that a person has only three choices when seeking to multiply money for God's glory. The idea applies whether someone has $10 or $100,000. Jesus' parables repeatedly mention all three options. The first is definitely to be avoided. The second, while better than the first, lacks the potential to bring the kind of increase the Bible says is possible. Both Old and New Testament characters alike utilized the third alternative in order to provide phenomenal returns.

The application works with money, such as the cash that might be in our checking or savings accounts. It also works with other resources—items that could be turned into cash if we wanted to do so. All three alternatives show up in Jesus' parable of the talents:

For the kingdom of heaven is like a man traveling to a far country, who called his own servants and delivered his goods to them. And to one he gave five talents, to another two, and to another one, to each according to his own ability; and immediately he went on a journey. Then he who had received the five talents went and traded with them, and made another five talents. And likewise he who had received two gained two more also. But he who had received one went and dug in the ground, and hid his lord's money. After a long time the lord of those servants came and settled accounts with them. So he who had received five talents came and brought five other talents, saying, "Lord, you delivered to me five talents; look, I have gained five more talents besides them." His lord said to him, "Well done, good and faithful servant; you were faithful over a few things, I will make you ruler over many things. Enter into the joy of your lord." He who had received two talents came and said, "Lord, you delivered to me two talents; look, I have gained two more talents besides them." His lord said to him, "Well done, good and faithful servant; you have been faithful over a few things, I will make you ruler over many things. Enter into the joy of your lord." Then he who had received the one talent came and said, "Lord, I knew you to be a hard man, reaping where you have not sown, and gathering where you have not scattered seed. And I was afraid, and went and hid your talent in the ground. Look, there you have what is yours." But his lord answered and said to him, "You wicked and lazy servant, you knew that I reap where I have not sown, and gather where I have not scattered seed. So you ought to have deposited my money with the bankers, and at my coming I would have received back my own with interest. There-

fore take the talent from him, and give it to him who has ten talents. For to everyone who has, more will be given, and he will have abundance; but from him who does not have, even what he has will be taken away" (Matthew 25:14-29).

The wealthy master in this parable obviously knows the importance of making a profit. These were "his own servants" (verse 14), presumably taught by him. We can suppose he had shared his experiences with them as they watched him make money. Now he took some of the money, entrusted it to them, and expected them to make a profit. Perhaps he thought, *They could expand the estate even further.*

This master called his servants together and gave one five talents. The word *talent* here does not refer to an ability, such as throwing a baseball or playing the piano. A *talent* was a sum of money like a piece of bullion. Various Bible dictionaries report that a talent of silver was worth anywhere from a thousand to a few hundred thousand dollars. Using the lower end of that range, you could guess that one steward received more than $5,000, another more than $2,000, and the other at least $1,000.

While the master was on his trip, the stewards who received the $5,000 and $2,000 each doubled their master's money. This accomplishment is impressive, whether today or in Jesus' day. The one-talent steward had more options than digging a hole in the ground to bury it. Among other options, he could have loaned it in order to gain interest.

Three Choices Available with Money

This master, upon his return, gathered the stewards together for a full accounting. Impressed with the first two, he gave them opportunity to make more profit in the future. They were faithful. Since they took a relatively small sum of money and did very well with it, the master promised a larger sum to work with the next time. They would have the chance to make even bigger profits in the future. Perhaps this cycle would be repeated again with even larger portions of his estate.

The man who received one talent came to the meeting but he apparently misunderstood his master's thought processes. His attitude was sort of like this: "Master, good news! Praise God, I didn't lose any." The master rebuked him, took the one talent from him, and gave it to the steward who had the most. The master then asked him one simple question: "Why didn't you at least take the money I gave you and place it somewhere it could have earned some interest?" The master's thinking was along the lines of "Wouldn't it be better to earn something than to earn nothing?" The master wasn't saying that it was the most profitable thing the servant could have done, only better.

From this parable comes the only three alternatives we have for managing and hopefully increasing resources or money. First, I can do the moral equivalent of burying my resources, just like the one-talent steward. The second path is slightly better. I could, as the master said to the one-talent man, "have deposited my money with the bankers and ... have received back my own with interest" (verse 27). The third alternative is worlds different in its results. It follows the spectacular example of the two men who doubled the master's money: "Then he who had received the five talents went and traded with them, and made another five talents" (verse 16). The word *traded* here, which describes what they did, may be a little unclear to us. It is not a word most people use. The NIV translation says, "put his money to work." The Living Bible reads, "The man... began to *buy* and *sell* with it and soon earned another $5,000" (emphasis added). Thus the final alternative for multiplying money is to use it in some fashion to buy and sell.

The master seems to have made much profit over the years. Perhaps he had learned how to recognize value. Maybe this was one of the skills he had taught his stewards. For all we know, the master mentored them on how to trade a previously undervalued investment, then they imitated him and did extremely well. Possibly he taught them how to recognize the impact of emotional forces in the marketplace. For example, fear pushes assets to an unsustainable low; greed pushes things to an unsustainable high. Neither of these forces can have a permanent upper hand. Whatever the case, their investment strategy appears to be ethical and legal, and the master gave them deserved praise upon receiving their return.

The Bible records a similar story in Luke. It contains the same parable, except that the stakes are now higher.

He said: "A man of noble birth went to a distant country to have himself appointed king and then to return. So he called ten of his servants and gave them ten minas. 'Put this money to work,' he said, 'until I come back.' But his subjects hated him and sent a delegation after him to say, 'We don't want this man to be our king.' He was made king, however, and returned home. Then he sent for the servants to whom he had given the money, in order to find out what they had gained with it. The first one came and said, 'Sir, your mina has earned ten more.' 'Well done, my good servant!' his master replied. 'Because you have been trustworthy in a very small matter, take charge of ten cities.' The second came and said, 'Sir, your mina has earned five more.' His master answered, 'You take charge of five cities.' Then another servant came and said, 'Sir, here is your mina; I have kept it laid away in a piece of cloth. I was afraid of you, because you are a hard man. You take out what you did not put in and reap what you did not sow.' His master replied, 'I will judge you by your own words, you wicked servant! You knew, did you, that I am a hard man, taking out what I did not put in, and reaping what I did not sow? Why then didn't you put my money on deposit, so that when I came back, I could have collected it with interest?' Then he said to those standing by, 'Take his mina away from him and give it to the one who has ten minas.' 'Sir,' they said, 'he already has ten!' He replied, 'I tell you that to everyone who has, more will be given, but as for the one who has nothing, even what he has will be taken away.'" (Luke 19:12-26 NIV).

It is important to know what a mina is. It is not a small sum of money. A mina is the equivalent of 100 days' wages. Whatever these men made for one day of work, the master multiplied it by 100 and gave them that much money at one time. It is more than a third of a year's pay. If you were to multiply your daily pay by 100, that would be a mina to you.

I have listened to conversations among Christians in which somebody mentions a large sum of money. Inevitably a brother would say, "You know, if I ever had that much money all at once, I sure don't know what I'd do with it." Looking back, I realize that has been part of our problem. What would you do if the Lord placed 100 days' wages in your hands at one time? You may respond first with a tithe and a generous offering beyond the 10 percent. Then what? That money is a candidate for multiplication.

I believe God's servants should know in our hearts what to do when resources are placed into our lives. It is not likely that the Master will place a large amount in our hands if we have no idea how to multiply His resources.

What to Do Until Jesus Comes

The King James Version of Luke 19:13 reads, "...occupy till I come." The word *occupy* has changed its meaning since Elizabethan times. When most people think of *occupy*, they see an image like sitting in a chair. In Jesus' day, however, the word was a business and commercial term.

The New King James Version translates verse 13 as, "Do business till I come." The New International Version says, "Put this money to work." I like the Amplified Bible, though. Its wording is the clearest of all. The master gave them ten minas and said, "Buy and sell with these while I go and return." Two of these stewards took this challenge to heart.

If the two double-your-money stewards in Matthew 25 were good, their two counterparts in Luke 19 are great. I call them the financial superstars of the whole Bible. They multiplied the master's money tenfold and fivefold, respectively. That level of return almost sounds like an ungodly profit, but yet the master said, "Well done, my good servant" (verse 17).

In dollars and cents, suppose a mina was $10,000. The first servant was saying, "I made $100,000 above the $10,000 you gave me." Wow! Yet their action must have been legal, honest, moral, and ethical. Otherwise Jesus would not have used it as a parable to communicate Kingdom truths. The man did not smuggle cocaine, but still returned 1,000 percent on the original investment.

A few years ago, a pastor from Arkansas told me a story that helped me relate to the huge scale of profit potential expressed in Luke 19. It also encouraged me that anyone can apply these principles, even people with traditionally low incomes, such as pastors.

This minister had listened to a tape on which I taught about these parables. The insights helped set him at ease regarding a previous transaction. Someone had offered to sell him 400,000 used bricks for 2 cents apiece. He made the purchase for a total outlay of $8,000. He told me, "Within a few months the Lord helped me sell every one of them for 20 cents apiece." He had turned $8,000 into $80,000— equaling a $72,000 profit. He made a ninefold profit, almost as much as the steward in chapter 19 of Luke.

Whenever you hear a story of this nature, remember that dollar amounts are not important. Whether we're talking about $8,000, $800, or $80, we must always come back to the three alternatives. You can do the equivalent of burying the money and make nothing. Or you can put the funds out for interest and earn a very small return. Interest is better than nothing, but it pales in comparison to a ten-fold multiplication.

In the Bible, whenever God speaks of money, He usually emphasizes the percent and not dollar amounts. According to the parable in Matthew 25, our reward as stewards will not be based on the dollar amounts, but on the percents. Whether the steward started with two or five units, the master was just as pleased. He rewarded them based on percents, not dollar amounts.

How to Identify Buried Resources

The example of this pastor shows the need to understand our choices when it comes to utilizing excess money. *Foolproof Finances* examines Scriptural reasons for why money flows to some people and away from others. It speaks of making Holy Spirit-directed changes in our lives from the wrong side to the positive side of God's promises. It next looks at God's plan to provide surplus, and it offers guidelines for using this excess money.

Is there a possibility that you, like one of those stewards, are burying valuable resources that God has entrusted to you? Granted, few people today stick $1,000 in a mattress or bury it in the backyard. However, we may possess things of value that we probably will not use before the second coming of Christ. Those resources are not increasing in value, nor are they adding benefit to our lives. After prayer, you may decide that your situation is the equivalent of burying that resource. You may be doing exactly the same thing as the steward in these parables who buried the talent or mina.

I am not referring to assets that add benefit to our lives. The dining room table and the couch are important for day-to-day living. If you have a rare coin, it may not be considered buried because it could be increasing in value. If you have an antique, it too would not be counted. It is probably increasing in value and even decorating some part of your home, and so adding benefit to your life.

Rather, you have perhaps stowed something away with no foreseen usage. You may be sitting here wondering why God has not provided anything to work with, and all the time you have more to work with than previously imagined.

I remember one farmer in Wisconsin. He said, "I was here on the farm and had all this junk laying around. I was going to give it away or otherwise get rid of it. It didn't seem valuable, but somebody finally talked me into having an auction." He held an auction solely to get rid of these items that he had planned to give away. He said, "Would you believe that I ended up with $24,000?" He probably thought he had nothing to work with, yet all the while he was sitting on a sizable treasure.

If you discover a resource in your life, that you determine is the equivalent of being buried, let me suggest three choices that would improve your stewardship of it. First, you could liquidate the resource into cash and give the entire proceeds as an offering to the Lord. As Jesus instructed his disciples, "Sell what you have and give to those in need. This will fatten your purses in heaven! And the purses of heaven have no rips or holes in them" (Luke 12:33a TLB). I do not believe the Lord would, in most cases, ask me to give the entire proceeds as an offering. I must simply seek His guidance on a daily basis.

Second, you could give a portion of the proceeds as an offering to the Lord. After that you might use the rest to reduce debt. That action would likewise show an improved stewardship over doing nothing.

There is a third alternative. After making an offering to the Lord, the balance of that money can become the seed for your financial deliverance. Here is an excellent case study that I learned in materials provided by Christian financial advisor Larry Burkett. I retell it with his permission. A missionary had been on the field for more than 40 years. Knowing that he would have mandatory retirement someday, he started setting money aside into his denomination's retirement plan. He earned interest on this money over the years. When he reached retirement age, he found out his retirement income would be $125 a month for the rest of his life. In the 1940's or 1950's, someone might live on $125 a month. In the 1980's, however, $125 a month could hardly pay the light bill. What would an individual in his 60's, facing mandatory retirement, do in that situation?

This missionary had the presence of mind and the leadership of the Holy Spirit to ask for help. He communicated his situation to Brother Burkett who probed the missionary for areas of special knowledge. Indeed, the missionary had accumulated a good deal of knowledge about Hummels—figurines made in Germany which just happen to be one of the top collectible items in the world. The missionary's study enabled him to know when a particular Hummel might be undervalued.

"Go home, search through your storage shed, your garage, and your attic," said Brother Larry. "Anything you don't need, liquidate it, turn it to cash, and then call me back." The missionary complied and assembled $1,800. The next step? "Take out an ad in the paper that says, 'I buy Hummels.' Include your number." The information this man accumulated over the years taught him how to recognize value in that area of investment. He took the $1,800 he had been able to put together and bought the Hummels that in his estimation were undervalued.

The retired missionary, on further counsel next took out a new ad that said, "I sell Hummels." People interested in collecting Hummels began to phone him. He repeated this process over and over again. The finale of the story was that the retired missionary later experienced an adjusted gross income of $256,00 for a one year period.

That investment opportunity did not come together overnight. It probably took a period of two to four years to happen. It started slow and built up to $256,000.

The resource was in that missionary's hand all the time. It had been buried. Then God used it as the seed for the man's financial deliverance. Similarly, the seed for your monetary freedom may already be in your hand, if you apply it differently than you are now and correctly.

Problems with Interest Rates

The second alternative suggested through Jesus' parables is that of earning interest on our resources. Nowhere does the Bible suggest that it is sinful to earn interest on our money, except possibly the Old Testament injunctions against making a profit off your poor brother (see Leviticus 25:35-37, Deuteronomy 23:19-20). No doubt you will have money on occasion that you need to park somewhere temporarily. A little interest is far better than no interest.

Most interest rates today lack the potential to produce the kind of financial blessings the Bible says are possible. That kind of engine simply cannot run fast enough. Take 1993, for example. The official inflation statistic was 2.6 percent. Suppose you could earn 3 percent on short-term money that year. Adjusted for inflation, your net gain would be 0.4 percent. After taxes, you might end up with less buying power than when you started. Nearly anyone in the financial world will tell you that on short-term money, you often earn a negative rate of return in today's world. Translation: you lose money every day. That approach is a far cry from something "pressed down, shaken together, and running over" (Luke 6:38).

Nothing Beats Buying and Selling

Jesus' parables present a third alternative. The master said, "Buy and sell with these while I go and then return" (Luke 19:13 AMP). In order to experience complete financial blessing in my lifetime, I must own things that increase in value. I have seen people increase their money supply in this way. All they need is to be perceptive, open to the Holy Spirit, and willing to apply the things they have learned.

I know a brother who went to a secular financial seminar. The essence of the conference was, "Here's what you should do with your first $100,000." I prefer stories that start with $25. I feel overwhelmed by investors who begin with $20,000 or $100,000. God's principles apply to the Christian with $100,000, but they are equally as valid with our first $100.

For example, I loved being a pastor and was well treated by the churches we served. However, at one point I realized that I clearly had a negative net worth. Due to lack of knowledge and training, far more money was flowing from me than to me. I began to make spiritual changes in order to get into the position where I had turned around. One adjustment involved receiving a personal benediction that matched my abilities and skills (this idea will be described later in this book). I learned that I served people better and fit more properly in traveling ministry than in the pastorate. That positioning allowed my finances to increase. Then over the past five or six years, my wife and I have purchased a couple of homes that were seriously undervalued due to peculiar economic circumstances (These homes were our personal dwellings.) One of these homes nearly doubled in value during the 3 years we lived there.

In August, 1992, most Christian economists were quite pessimistic. They advised listeners to divest themselves of any stocks or stock mutual funds before the fall Presidential elections. By contrast, I began to feel in my heart that all major stock indexes would reach all-time highs in 1993. I came to believe that the Lord wanted me to shift my small retirement account from a very conservative approach to the most aggressive stock fund offered by my fund family. Placing that phone call took all the courage I could muster, but the results have been very rewarding. When I left that aggressive fund in January, 1994, I had advanced by 70 percent on the money that I had invested over seventeen months earlier.

Recently, in watching the news, I became convinced that the price of cattle had bottomed out. So I picked up a trio of calves, which my sons are now raising. They are increasing in value as of this writing, and when sold will turn into a profit. Not everyone has five acres, but every believer does possess talents and circumstances that can be increased for God's glory.

One pastor in Kansas told me about a congregation member who knew something about antique toys. He would go to a garage sale or an auction and, knowing what was undervalued, buy antique toys for $25 or $30 apiece. He had contacts with people who appreciated antique toys. They would then buy these items for $300 or $400 each, resulting in a tenfold increase.

The profit from one such transaction would not support a missionary for one year. Nor would it fund an orphanage. However, what were his alternatives? If he buries that $25, he earns nothing. If he put the $25 out for interest, in one year's time at 3 percent, he would have earned 75 cents. Granted, 75 cents is better than zero. However, it pales in comparison to $300 or $400.

Another man from Missouri made his living as a carpenter. After hearing the teachings in this book, a mobile home came up for sale in his vicinity. For unknown reasons, the price at which it was offered was greatly under the value he saw in the property. The carpenter realized this bargain thanks to his knowledge of property values. He and his wife had little extra money to work with, but they re-

membered the parable of the talents. They remembered that
the master said to his stewards, "I want you to buy and sell
until I get back." They went to the bank and arranged to
borrow the money to buy the mobile home. Within three
weeks of the purchase, they sold the trailer house and realized a $10,000 profit. They used the proceeds to pay off the
mortgage on their home and become more debt-free. Their
action opened up another avenue of income into their lives.

Similar stories come from Scripture as well. Here is
an instance from the life of Solomon.

*And Solomon had horses imported from Egypt and
Keveh; the king's merchants bought them in Keveh at
the current price. Now a chariot that was imported from
Egypt cost six hundred shekels of silver, and a horse
one hundred and fifty; and thus, through their agents,
they exported them to all the kings of the Hittites and
the kings of Syria* (I Kings 10:28-29).

Solomon was buying horses and chariots in Egypt.
He turned around and sold them to a group of heathen kings.
Without a doubt, Solomon was making a profit on these
heathen kings. The wealth of the wicked was coming to the
righteous, as Solomon himself described in Proverbs 13:22b:
"a sinner's wealth is stored up for the righteous" (NIV). In
Scripture, when the wealth of the wicked transfers to the
righteous, it usually occurs through legitimate transactions
in the marketplace. Solomon's export business is one such
example.

Practical Applications

If every believer will put the concepts in this chapter to work, the Body of Christ will deliver a cumulative knock-out punch to the devil's devices. Here are a number of practical places to put some money, in addition to the examples already cited.

First, invest in your own skills or business. Planned carefully, this process will produce a safe return in the quickest possible time. For instance, if you are certain that a computer or other particular piece of equipment could directly increase your income, then consider investing your money in this way. The risk here would be very low.

Second, you probably have money you want to put toward your later years on this earth, if the Lord tarries. Most Christian economists recommend putting those funds into an IRA within a growth-stock mutual fund. These types of funds buy and sell the shares of the world's or the United States' most promising companies. Some of these types of funds have averaged between 15-18 percent over 20- to 40-year periods. This subject deserves to be researched at your local library.

Third, make your home a profitable investment. In buying any future home, consider only those situations likely to appreciate in value over the next three to five years. Again, your local library can be a great resource.

Fourth, invest in other areas where you have the ability to recognize value.

In Summary

Six basic principles stand out in the stewardship parables of Matthew 25 and Luke 19. First, our Master is successful and wants to teach us how to be likewise. "Thus says the Lord, your Redeemer, the Holy One of Israel: 'I am the Lord your God, who teaches you to profit...'" (Isaiah 48:17).

Second, the use of money to buy and sell is a heavenly approved way of increasing prosperity. God will not be against it as long as I do not violate other divine principles along the way. For example, if I lied or extorted someone in order to achieve a gain, then my profit will not please God. If my heart is greedy, selfish, or arrogant, then my prosperity did not come in the will of God.

A third principle involves the Christian's need to act as a top-flight steward, not an owner. All money is the Lord's. If we make a profit, both it and the money are still His. At the least, I should get interest on his resources. Even better, I should learn about value and seeing opportunity. When I make a mistake and suffer a loss, all I have is still the Lord's. I am His steward.

Fourth, it is the master's responsibility to put something in the steward's hands to work with. In the parable he did not say to the men, "Do you have any money?" He took his money and placed it in their hands. Thus the master's responsibility is to remind me of what I already have that needs to be unburied. Or He will put some new resource in my hands.

Fifth, my responsibility is to increase my ability. The master put money in the steward's hands, "to each according to his own ability" (Matthew 25:15). I do not need to identify a top-notch investment opportunity by first thing tomorrow morning. Rather, my top priority is to sharpen my abilities. The more I increase these, the more attractive it becomes for the master to put something in my hands with which to work.

Sixth and finally, motives are important to God. When the steward reported, "Master, your mina...," he was referring to profits for the master's use. His motive did not seem to focus on luxury or what he would get out of the deal. This servant noticeably differs from the farmer who made large profits, planned to build bigger barns, and then said to himself, "Soul, you have many goods laid up for many years to come" (see Luke 12:18-19). God's response to him was, "Fool! This night your soul will be required of you" (Luke 12:20). What a far cry from, "Well done, good servant..." (Luke 19:17). Both made profit, but one was for the master's use. Even so, the steward with the pure motives was probably rewarded with a higher standard of living (see Luke 19:17, 19). A rising standard of living can be consistent with pure motives.

Everyone is at a different place both spiritually and financially. A few can step out with the information from this chapter and begin reaping profits. Others will allow this information to remain on file in their hearts. At a later date, the Lord will use it to bring in a bountiful harvest.

I close this chapter with several admonitions. These are vital if you ever intend to profit in the fashion described in this chapter.

First, as a way of increasing your ability, seek out those in your circle of Christian friends who have made money either unexpectedly or deliberately. Proverbs 13:20a says, "He who walks with wise men will be wise." Glean understanding from them. Ask, "How did you know that item was undervalued? How did you learn that? What did you read?" By so doing you become a candidate for the master to put resources in your hands.

Second, allow God to work with you to build up a surplus. Liquidate any resources that are the equivalent of being buried. Discipline yourself to set aside money regularly, even if it is a small amount. Believe God for resources to work with. A Christian banker once told me there have been times he could have bought a dollar for 50 cents, figuratively speaking, but was unable to do so. He simply had no reserve to work with. Without any reserve, opportunity can knock on your door and you will not be able to answer.

Third, do not strive to get rich quick. Proverbs warns us several times against such tactics. I propose this alternative: do a little better this year than you did last year. If every Christian did so, the increased tithes and offerings would have a significant impact on global worldwide evangelism.

As you move toward financial freedom, do not assume that you must struggle each step of the way. Enjoy the journey and the learning experiences it provides. Most of all, enjoy Jesus each and every day.

Questions

1. Name a specific resource that you consider to be buried right now. What will you do to put it to work?

2. In what types of assets or items are you able to recognize value? Be specific.

3. What friend or acquaintance is equipped to teach you how to profit? When can you next meet with this person?

Key Action Points:

I. Identify your resources that are presently buried (special skills, knowledge, potential assets not in use, etc.)

II. Consider three good uses for your money that is presently buried
    1. Give to the Lord
    2. Pay down debt
    3. Use to Increase

III. Ask the Lord for wisdom in increasing the resources He has already given you

IV. Seek practical ways to turn toward a favorable position for increase:
    1. Invest in your own skills and abilities
    2. Invest in areas where you have the ability to recognize value
    3. Make your home a profitable investment

Chapter 5

Five Sequences of Biblical Increase

Perhaps the greatest financial promise in the Bible appears in the Apostle Paul's letter to the Philippians. He wrote, "My God shall supply all your need according to His riches in glory by Christ Jesus" (Philippians 4:19). Woven inside this wonderful promise is also a great challenge.

Everyone has certain types of tangible needs. Maybe your need is for employment. Perhaps your car has become like the old gospel song—it "went the last mile of the way." Possibly you live in a two-bedroom house, but because you have helped "multiply and replenish the earth" (Genesis 1:28 KJV), your family could easily fill a four or five bedroom home.

Exchanging Heavenly for Tangible

God says He will do something about your needs. He promises to supply them with His riches in glory. God's provision is just as real, or perhaps more real, than your need.

However, God's riches in glory come from a different dimension. He is saying, "I'll meet your need in the earthly realm with riches that are over here in the heavenly realm." The believer's challenge is to draw riches from the heavenly sphere into the earthly domain.

Suppose I am in Texas. My pocket contains a large roll of Canadian one-hundred dollar bills. Since I have so much money, I invite a huge number of friends out for dinner. After they leave the restaurant, I go to the cash register to pay the bill. There I discover a big problem: all my Canadian cash cannot buy one Texan hamburger. The money is real, but it comes from another realm. I can benefit from it only if I exchange it first.

The same idea applies to God's riches in glory. They are real. However, they cannot benefit me materially unless I first exchange them into something usable in my present realm.

I believe such an exchange process exists. It consists of five sequences. These steps display themselves over and over throughout the Old and the New Testaments. As a result, the process seems to be a deeply established procedure from God's Word. It allows us to exchange wealth from the spiritual domain into something tangible. It can lead to a powerful, abundant flow of financially related provision.

More Than Unexpected Cash in the Mailbox

Many Christians limit themselves by believing stereotypes of how God provides for financial needs. For example, one commonly expressed perception says Christians walk into the church building, put tithes and offerings into the storehouse there, go home, and then all kinds of money will one day show up in their mailbox. "God said He will open the windows of Heaven," they say, "so maybe this is how the increase will fall on us."

Certainly God does inspire such gifts in the mailbox, especially in instances of urgent, critical need. For example, suppose a person is doing everything possible, but is still cut back on his or her hours at work. A utility bill comes due for $50. God could prompt a saint to slip $55 under this individual's door. Five dollars can be a tithe to the Lord and the remaining $50 will pay the utility bill. The gift will cover the need, but nothing more. Such provision may be divinely orchestrated, but it does not fully represent the exchange process of Biblical increase.

Additionally, God sometimes inspires people to offer generous help with ministry projects that God has laid on your heart. Christians may rally around your vision and help supply the funds you need. Again the need will be met, but not in a multiplied fashion.

The following five steps show another pathway by which God meets needs. In the process, he also fulfills certain huge, enormous Bible promises.

Five Sequences of God's Increase

First the Lord asks us to give. This first phase should not surprise anyone. Jesus unashamedly asks his followers to give to Himself. He even asked for a little boy's lunch (see John 6:9-11). Jesus boldly and confidently, with no reservation or hesitation, can ask us to present back to Him a portion of what He has blessed us with. Jesus does so because He plans to do something benevolent with it. With the boy's lunch, he fed a crowd of 5,000 people. With our gifts today, he likewise uses them for good.

Second, God opens the windows of heaven. The prophet Malachi says that once we present our tithe as well as offerings to the Lord, He opens the windows of heaven.

> *"Bring all the tithes into the storehouse, that there may be food in My house, and try Me now in this," says the Lord of hosts, "if I will not open for you the windows of heaven and pour out for you such blessing that there will not be room enough to receive it"* (Malachi 3:10).

I do not fully understand the phrase, *windows of heaven.* Maybe it means something opens in my spirit, heart, and mind so that I can hear the voice of God more clearly than ever before. Or possibly more spiritual light can now come into my life than before, since a window lets light in. Whatever the case, something called the "windows of heaven" are now open because I responded to the Lord's invitation to give.

Third, once that window opens, God begins to speak either "an idea, a concept, an opportunity, or wisdom"[1] *that*

---

[1] I have adopted this phrase from the teachings of Larry Lea. His writings include *Could You Not Tarry One Hour* (Lake Mary, FL: Strang Communications, 1987); *The Hearing Ear: Learning to Listen to God* (Lake Mary, FL: Strang Communications, 1990); *Highest Calling: Serving in the Royal Priesthood* (Lake Mary, FL: Strang Communications, 1991); and *Weapons of Warfare* (Lake Mary, FL: Strang Communications, 1989).

fits my life perfectly. (We will examine that concept in greater detail later.)

Fourth, I must act on God's word for me. I need to do something with it. I must put this word into motion, whether it is an idea, a concept, an opportunity, or wisdom. Whatever comes through that window is designed to help me reach the goals of life that God has planned for me.

Fifth, God releases a flow of finances. More finances come into my life than anything I have experienced to date. The natural processes of life now move financial favor toward me as I obey God and follow through on the blessings of the open window.

Peter Experienced the Sequence

The Bible illustrates this sequence of divine blessing in Luke 5.

One day as Jesus was standing by the Lake of Gennesaret, with the people crowding around Him and listening to the word of God, He saw at the water's edge two boats, left there by the fishermen, who were washing their nets. He got into one of the boats, the one belonging to Simon, and asked him to put out a little from shore. Then He sat down and taught the people from the boat. When He had finished speaking, He said to Simon, "Put out into deep water, and let down the nets for a catch." Simon answered, "Master, we've worked hard all night and haven't caught anything. But because You say so, I will let down the nets." When they had done so, they caught such a large number of fish that their nets began to break. So they sig-

naled their partners in the other boat to come and help them, and they came and filled both boats so full that they began to sink (Luke 5:1-7 NIV).

In this situation, Jesus is ministering to thousands of people. Everyone wants to get closer to Him. They want to see and hear Him better. They push through the crowd, bringing their sick children to Jesus. As a result, they squeeze Jesus against the lake.

Jesus knew that in order to keep doing what He does best, He must have a platform. Because of that need, He turned to a man named Simon. In essence, Jesus asked the man who would become the Apostle Peter to borrow his boat.

Simon Peter now has an opportunity to sow a seed into the ministry of Jesus. Peter has probably heard all the good things that Jesus had been doing—healing the sick, cleansing the lepers, raising the dead, and casting out demons. Who in his right mind would not want to help Jesus? The Bible gives no clue that Peter resisted. Nor did he reply, "The boat rents for $50 an hour and my time is worth $25 an hour. You'll need this for at least two hours, so that's $150. And in keeping with Your hundredfold-return ideas, that will be $15,000, please." Instead, Peter seemed happy to help.

When Simon Peter gave Jesus use of his boat, he was bringing an offering to the storehouse. The boat was the best thing he had to offer Jesus. It represented his business and livelihood. It was perhaps his most valuable possession. What better storehouse than the ministry of Jesus, who met people's physical and spiritual needs every day?

Peter appears to have effectively engaged Malachi 3:10. As a result, the windows of heaven were about to open on Simon Peter. If he had a money-in-the-mailbox stereotype, he might have expected schools of fish to jump out of the water and cascade into his boat. First they would fill the boat where Jesus stood and then they would leap into his second boat.

Instead, Jesus told Simon to let out his net in the deep for a catch of fish. This inspired word from God to Simon was the illumination of divine guidance. Its intent was to bring blessing on Simon because of how he faithfully invested in the ministry of Jesus. Jesus' word came through the "open windows" mentioned in Malachi 3:10.

The word *blessing* in Malachi 3:10 is not a direct reference to money. According to *Strong's Concordance,*[2] it primarily means "benediction." Broken down grammatically, this word comes from *bene* and *diction. Bene* means good. *Diction* is a flow of words. Webster's Dictionary defines benediction as "to speak well of."[3] Therefore, God is making this promise: "I'll open the windows of heaven and pour out for you a benediction—through the windows of heaven will start a flow of words that are good."

Jesus Gave Peter a Benediction

When Jesus said to Simon Peter, "Put out into deep water, and let down the nets for a catch" (Luke 5:4 NIV), that statement was a benediction for him. It was an idea

---

[2] #1293 in James Strong, *The Exhaustive Concordance of the Bible.* (Peabody, MA: Hendrickson Publishers, n.d.).
[3] *Webster's Ninth New Collegiate Dictionary.* (Springfield, MA: Merriam-Webster, 1985).

that fit his life perfectly. Simon Peter was a fisherman by trade. What God said through that window just happened to be about fishing!

Peter could respond in many different ways. Either he will apply the illumination to a onetime possibility or he might see a whole new way of doing business. Catching fish in the deep part represented a new concept. Fishermen on the Sea of Galilee historically fished at night and in the shallow part of the lake. That approach is probably how Peter had always fished, along with his father and grandfather before him. His friends no doubt fished in a similar way. It was possibly the only way they understood fishing.

They had no idea that someone could go to the deep part of the lake in the daytime and catch fish. Suddenly Peter's thinking shifts about the fishing business. If this word represented a new way of doing business, he could end up the most prosperous fisherman along the Sea of Galilee.

When Peter received this benediction, Malachi 3:10 was being fulfilled. Peter gave, the windows opened, and God began pouring out a benediction. The phrase *pour out* tells me that God will start saying it and keep saying it. Those words flow through our spirits and occasionally one of them will stick! God's wisdom comes from a never-ending supply.

Listening for Your Benediction

I spent a portion of my life trying to believe God for what I *thought* He promised. It is usually easier, however, to believe Him for exactly what He promises and not what we thought He has said. He has specifically promised to deliver a word with the potential to change our financial situation.

I do not have to hear everything God is saying through that window. I need only one tiny fragment of information in the benediction to change my life. Perhaps I could not even handle the whole benediction; it is coming from the depth of the mind of God.

Paul described God's benedictions this way: "Oh, the depth of the riches both of the wisdom and knowledge of God!" (Romans 11:33a). That verse describes the pool from which this benediction is drawn. Financial increase means getting a fragment of information from that benediction from time to time. Each fragment can bring in more finances than anything I have experienced up to that point.

Having heard the benediction, what did Peter have to do next? He had to act on it. Peter says:

"Master, we have toiled all night and caught nothing; nevertheless at Your word I will let down the net." And when they had done this, they caught a great number of fish, and their net was breaking. So they signaled to their partners in the other boat to come and help them. And they came and filled both the boats, so that they began to sink" (Luke 5:5-7).

This is an exciting story. Peter takes out the first boat, and the nets go over the side. They started hauling in huge loads of fish. He was probably stunned at their success. He completely filled his boat. If you had seen Peter then, you probably would have called him "Mr. Enthusiasm."

91

Peter knew how many pounds of fish his boat would hold. He also knew the value of these fish. Historically, fish caught on the Sea of Galilee were of such good quality that they were dried, salted, and exported all over the Roman Empire. Since this was Peter's business, he must have known the current market price. Possibly Peter was crunching the numbers in his mind as he pulled in the fish.

Do you know what else he was excited about? He had another boat. I can see him in my mind, standing in the front of that first boat, waving his arms excitedly and shouting, "You've got to get the other boat out here now!"

Peter looked over the side of the first boat after it was full. He knew more fish were down there. The second boat came out and it filled too. I believe Peter looked over the side of both full boats and saw even more fish. He did not have room enough to contain the blessing. The sequence was Malachi 3:10 fulfilled exactly.

This story illustrates God's promise. When someone tithes, the windows will open and a flow of words will come through. What I must do then, with the aid and help of the Holy Spirit, is begin pulling life application from that benediction. When that benediction came through the windows, Peter was not alone. Jesus was there to help him extract the fragments that pertained to his life.

Jesus said, "I will not leave you comfortless.... I will ... give you another Comforter" (John 14:16,18 KJV). The Holy Spirit is that *other* Comforter. He will do the same kind of things inside us that Jesus did when He walked the earth. The Holy Spirit working inside us is primed and ready to help us draw from the portions of the benediction that pertain to you and me.

God's benedictions help us transcend the natural. The obstacle against Peter was his limited understanding of the fishing business. He did not know about new places full of fish. This benediction lifted him above his natural understanding and enabled him to catch an extraordinary amount. The fish had probably been there for some time; Peter simply had not known how to catch them.

Do Christians lack money because so little of it exists? Of course not. All around us are huge amounts of resources. We simply do not see how to tap into them. God's benediction serves to draw together our skills, abilities, and characteristics, and focus them in a meaningful direction. They will then be arranged in the right order. The abilities you already possess will begin producing more income than they do presently. We do not have to become someone we are not in order to do better financially.

Jacob Also Received a Benediction

Another instance of this principle being fulfilled occurred in the life of Jacob. His grandfather, Abraham, was quite wealthy. His father, Isaac, was actually wealthier than Abraham. The Bible says that Abraham gave all that he had to Isaac (see Genesis 25:5). Then Isaac added to Abraham's fortune. Jacob grew up in an atmosphere of wealth and apparently desired to be wealthy. However, Jacob had one of those character flaws referred to in Chapter 2 of this book. God's covenant required a removal of this flaw before Jacob could walk in the promised blessings of Abraham.

Jacob's character flaw caused him to engage in a get-rich-quick scheme at his brother's expense. His brother, Esau, being the firstborn, possessed the birthright. In those days, a birthright meant he would receive twice as much inheritance as any of the other sons. Since Isaac had two sons, Esau would receive two-thirds of Isaac's fortune and Jacob one-third. The total inheritance, in today's currency, was probably into the millions.

Genesis 25:29-34 tells about one day when Esau came home from hunting. He was exhausted and famished. Jacob had made a pot of stew and Esau requested some. Jacob saw his chance. He said, "I'll give you some stew in exchange for your birthright."

Jacob's character flaws blinded him to perspectives that should have been obvious. Thirty minutes later, Esau will not think his trade was such a great deal. As a result, he will seek vengeance. That million-dollar bowl of soup must have been the most expensive meal in history. Esau, as a hunter, was probably big, strong, and muscular. He was good with a bow, arrow, and spear. If you are going to cheat anybody, an athlete like that is the wrong person. This example shows why the Father cleanses us before He prospers us; otherwise uncorrected faults cause deep trouble later on.

Jacob was blinded and could not look at these events rationally. All he could see was the money. Events like these made Esau furious. He started threatening Jacob's life. He said in effect, "When Isaac, our father, dies, I am going to kill Jacob" (see Genesis 27:41). As a result, Jacob had to leave home. The Bible tells us he departed with nothing more than his staff (see Genesis 32:10). Jacob was now at a place of starting over. Many Christians have likewise started at that point.

Look at Jacob's emotional roller coaster. He appeared to have doubled his inheritance from one-third to two-thirds of Isaac's fortune. Everything looked good. He appeared set for life with an inheritance worth millions in today's terms. However, in a short while, he fled his home penniless. He had gone from the very top to the very bottom.

Still, God met Jacob in that condition. Notice that God's visit occurred not at Jacob's best, but at his worst. God seems to enjoy making Himself known when someone deserves it the least. Following the five-sequence pattern of increase, Jacob now has a Holy Spirit-inspired dream. Here is his response:

Then Jacob made a vow, saying, "If God will be with me, and keep me in this way that I am going, and give me bread to eat and clothing to put on, so that I come back to my father's house in peace, then the Lord shall be my God. And this stone which I have set as a pillar shall be God's house, and of all that You give me I will surely give a tenth to You" (Genesis 28:20-22).

Jacob made a threefold commitment to the Lord. He made a spiritual commitment when he said, "The Lord will be my God." He made a commitment to a place of worship. He said, "This stone... shall be God's house." Third, he made a financial commitment: "All that You give me, I will surely give a tenth to You." Once he made this commitment, including that third part concerning the tithe, he

95

brought upon himself the promise of Malachi that the windows of heaven will open.

Jacob's Benediction Came Through a Dream

At a later time, Jacob received another Holy Spirit-inspired dream that gave him his benediction. Jacob worked for Laban in return for the privilege of marrying Laban's daughters. At the end of that particular obligation, Jacob had a dream. It occurred during the events described in chapter 30; then he told his wives about it during the sequence of Genesis 31.

And it happened, at the time when the flocks conceived, that I lifted my eyes and saw in a dream, and behold, the rams which leaped upon the flocks were streaked, speckled, and gray-spotted. Then the Angel of God spoke to me in a dream, saying, "Jacob." And I said, "Here I am." And He said, "Lift your eyes now and see, all the rams which leap on the flocks are streaked, speckled, and gray-spotted; for I have seen all that Laban is doing to you. I am the God of Bethel, where you anointed the pillar and where you made a vow to Me. Now arise, get out of this land, and return to the land of your family" (Genesis 31:10-13).

It is no coincidence that God spoke to Jacob about sheep. Jacob was a shepherd. Because those windows of heaven were open, a benediction comes. Through the vehicle of a dream, God helped Jacob comprehend something that would greatly change his finances. He was now positioned for those blessings of Abraham.

Jacob began to see a whole new way of doing business. The idea, as applied, would cause a transfer of wealth. Some of Laban's wealth would go to Jacob. Laban worshipped idols and false gods, and the Bible says that men like him lay up their wealth for the just (see Proverbs 13:22). If God wants to transfer His money from a wicked man to a righteous man, He has every right to do so.

God was apparently showing Jacob something about a biological law governing reproduction and heredity. He was also giving him a master strategy for putting that information to work in a beneficial way. I wish the Bible gave us a little more detail on this dream. Perhaps it was more clear to Jacob. Nevertheless, his response was to act on God's benediction.

So he said, "What shall I give you?" And Jacob said, "You shall not give me anything. If you will do this thing for me, I will again feed and keep your flocks: Let me pass through all your flock today, removing from there all the speckled and spotted sheep, and all the brown ones among the lambs, and the spotted and speckled among the goats; and these shall be my wages" (Genesis 30:31-32).

Notice which sheep Jacob negotiated for as wages. Those are exactly the same ones he saw in the dream. He was putting into motion what he had seen.

Now Jacob took for himself rods of green poplar and of the almond and chestnut trees, peeled white strips in them, and exposed the white which was in the rods. And the rods which he had peeled, he set before the flocks in the gutters, in the watering troughs where the flocks came to drink, so that they should conceive when they came to drink. So the flocks conceived before the rods, and the flocks brought forth streaked, speckled, and spotted (Genesis 30:37-39).

In those days, white lambs were the most desirable. Laban had arranged with Jacob that every baby lamb born pure white would be Laban's. Every baby lamb born spotted, speckled, or streaked would be Jacob's. Laban, however, made a deal with someone who had "inside information." Jacob utilized those rods and affected how the sheep interacted and reproduced. Every time those rods were placed in or near the watering troughs, the future baby lambs were born spotted, speckled, or streaked. Therefore, they all belonged to Jacob.

Thus the man became exceedingly prosperous, and had large flocks, female and male servants, and camels and donkeys (Genesis 30:43).

Verses 37 through 43 take place over a six-year period. That fact also provides us with insight. Since Proverbs warns us at least five times against getting rich quickly, under most circumstances it is not God's will to dump lots of money on us suddenly.

Improvements Should Start Immediately

I believe it is God's desire, however, that our finances begin improving immediately. He would like things to be better next week. He would like for our pressure to ease. Some of that strain would lift if we simply implemented a few principles for managing and budgeting our money.

Also, if you have not been presenting 10 percent of your increase to the Lord, your finances will improve if you begin to do so now. If a believer does not present the appropriate portion to the Lord, a lack of spiritual rightness results. This condition opens the door for confusion. Because of this disorder, I believe a person will waste more than the 10 percent he or she would have given to the Lord. When that rightness clicks in and the confusion lifts, the believer will all of a sudden see more clearly than ever before. He or she will also become a wiser spender, getting more mileage out of the 90 percent left than formerly from the full 100 percent.

In a way, everybody tithes. The question is to which god the tithe goes. By an act of will I can tithe to the God of heaven. By default I can give to the god of self-indulgence. Tithing to the Lord allows me to redeem the ten percent that would most probably have been lost anyway. I will also receive numerous spiritual and financial blessings in the process.

When Jacob received those first sheep from Laban, his net worth immediately improved. He was not rich yet, but his wealth grew as those sheep had baby lambs. Those sheep had more baby lambs, and the process continued until Jacob's finances hit an exponential curve in only a few years. (An exponential curve is a line that starts rising gradually, and then curves in a rapid upward direction.) In six years Jacob went from earning wages and meeting his basic needs to becoming exceedingly prosperous. Jacob's experience and the above time frames are a great lesson to all believers.

One Man's Benediction Involved Skateboarding

Here is a story about a brother who belonged to the church I pastored in Missouri. At the time I was only starting to learn a few of the ideas behind *Foolproof Finances*. I do not take any credit for what happened. The best thing I did was not get in faith's way!

This man was in his mid-twenties and a carpenter by trade. He had no educational or financial advantages over anyone reading this book. He worked hard. He earned his hourly wages. He met his bills. But he was not yet experiencing God's overflowing blessing.

Being a consistent tither, this believer had a flow of God's words coming through the windows of heaven to him. One day he heard a fragment of the benediction: "You need to build a skateboard park."

That wisdom fit his life perfectly. As a teen he had lived in the mountains. He and his friends would take their skateboards to the top of a mountain and ride them down the mountain highway. So he had a good idea of how to design the park.

His personality also contained a magnetism that attracted teenagers. He liked them and enjoyed working with them. Being a carpenter he knew how to build the obstacle course, ramps, and other props. The ability to do these things himself no doubt saved hundreds to thousands of dollars, eliminating a deterrent to the project. Thus God, with one fragment of a benediction, pulled together these disconnected elements and arranged them in a better order. The park opened and in a few months God sent him more than

1,000 teenagers. Each paid monthly dues to be a member. Income also came in from the sale of refreshments, pads, helmets, skateboards, and shoes.

The park eventually served about 2,000 teenagers. In less than one year we saw a brother go from earning hourly wages to receiving a multi-thousand-dollar-a-month cash flow. God's idea released more finances into his life than anything he had experienced up to that point.

God always has a way of weaving in spiritual opportunities as well. This man had an evangelistic call on his life. He was always trying to find ways to tell teenagers about Jesus. With the skateboard park, he had up to 2,000 teens coming to him, paying him money while he told them about Jesus. That is what I call witnessing on a grand scale. I stand amazed at how this particular benediction drew together both the spiritual and the financial sides of life. The potential of a divine benediction is incredibly far-reaching.

God Still Uses Dreams Today

This chapter has highlighted the role of a benediction in the Biblical pattern of increase. In order to convey His benediction to us, God has several delivery vehicles waiting in the wings. As I come into fuller obedience to the Lord Jesus and my finances start coming into divine order, then I am ready to hear. Sometimes the delivery vehicle is an inward witness; sometimes it is the clear, distinguishable voice of the Holy Spirit. If necessary, God also has the vehicles of visions and dreams (see Acts 2:17) to get His word to us. God's practice is to deliver benedictions that perfectly fit a person's life.

I had the opportunity to minister in the church where a certain individual attended. This man tithes generously to the Lord's work out of a heart that delights in giving. He purchased a set of my teaching tapes and reviewed them several times. He was intrigued by the fact that God literally gave Jacob a dream.

This brother was a real estate developer in Georgia and was in the midst of a financial downturn. One day God impressed upon him an internal picture affecting his vocation. It was so strong it can be compared to Jacob's dream. In this picture he saw soil maps that had the city limits of his town drawn on it. Later, he assembled soil maps and marked the city limits on them. Then, within those boundaries, he colored in each lot that already had a building on it. Using another color he filled in each lot that was designated as a wetland. (This type of property cannot be developed without a special permit.) Upon completion, his enhanced soil map revealed the lots available for development inside the city limits. To his amazement there were relatively few that could be built upon.

This God-given picture came to him during the time of Operation Desert Storm. The Army had deployed the division from a nearby military base, causing thousands of soldiers to ship out to the Middle East. Typically, such departures hit a local economy hard; real estate prices usually drop significantly. This scenario occurred, making most of the lots available to be purchased at an undervalued price. This brother secured an option to buy most of them for a designated price within a set time.

In the meantime he took his map to the mayor and city council, who had previously voted against annexing more land into the city. When they saw how little property was available for development within the city, they soon annexed more. The first land they annexed was 600 acres that this man owned right outside town. Immediately that property value increased by five times.

My friend soon learned that the Army Corps of Engineers had an easement through the 600 acres to build a road. They wanted to build a road on the edge of the property, but the surveyors had forgotten to record the easement. As a result, he was able to require the Corps of Engineers to build the road down the middle of his property. He received a wonderful paved road with a sewer line underneath and sidewalks on both sides. This remarkable event saved him many thousands of dollars.

When Kuwait was liberated, the Army sent this division home at 120 percent strength, not the 80 percent strength at departure. The community now had thousands more soldiers than before. Previously the emotion of fear had driven real estate prices ridiculously low. Now the emotion of greed pushed prices very high. Cash flow for this brother went way up. Thus his dream soon led to other opportunities.

Balancing Internal and External Prosperity

This testimony highlights how a benediction both fits our lives and leads to increase. It also demonstrates God's ability to deliver a word through various means. God is no respecter of persons. He delights in giving good gifts to all His children.

Why would God establish the pattern described in this chapter? He can dump large amounts of money on anyone He wants. I believe the answer shows God's concern for our ongoing maturity in Christ. What He says through those windows changes me on the inside first; then it flows out and starts changing me financially. That sequence enables me to stay in line with III John 2: "Beloved, I pray that you may prosper in all things and be in health, just as your soul prospers." The benediction that comes through the windows causes my soul to prosper. Then, as I put God's good word into motion, it causes me to prosper additionally on the outside. In this way, my external prosperity never exceeds my internal prosperity.

Money has incredibly seductive power. It is hard for a rich person to enter the kingdom of God (see Mark 10:25). The temptation to love money or trust in riches can corrupt even a mature believer. For this reason, Christians are in a dangerous spot whenever their external income exceeds their internal prosperity. The tension between the two gives the devil an advantage in putting pressure on that person.

Perhaps you have been disillusioned because you have given wholeheartedly to God's work in the past but have not seen noticeable improvement in your financial condition. You need to forget those things that are behind. Today you can begin believing God for *what* He promised, not for what you *thought* He promised. Just as Jacob lifted his eyes and expected to see something (see Genesis 31:10), so you must anticipate that the Holy Spirit will communicate a benediction to you through all the different vehicles available to Him. You will see something that fits your life.

It will start lifting you out of the place where you are. It will start releasing more finances into your life.

Questions

1. What are you doing to open the windows of Heaven in your life?

2. What idea has God already been speaking to you?

3. What is your equivalent of Jacob's dream?

Key Action Points:

I. Remember the Five Steps or Sequences of Biblical Increase
   1. The Lord asks us to give
   2. The windows of heaven open
   3. An idea, concept, opportunity, or wisdom that fits your life perfectly comes through the window
   4. You act on the idea
   5. A flow of blessing is released

II. Examine where you are in the sequence

III. Take appropriate action

Chapter 6

Legitimate Ways to Multiply Kingdom Money[1]

Before a highway department builds a new street, workers conduct traffic studies to determine how many lanes need to be created. They want to know how many cars will use the road each day. The more lanes they make, the more traffic can pass on the road. A little-used route needs only two lanes. A busier street may need a special lane for turning in the middle. A major thoroughfare might require four lanes. For congestion on a scale of rush hour in Los Angeles, perhaps ten lanes will barely suffice.

Imagine a town that has only two-lane streets, yet all the traffic from downtown Los Angeles needs to pass through. A big problem will occur; traffic will back up for miles.

[1] Some inspiration and material for this chapter is drawn from Bill Gothard's *Men's Manual*, Volume II, Revised Edition, June 1984, 3rd Printing. (Oak Brook, IL: Institute in Basic Life Principles).

As ridiculous as that scenario is, believers often try to do the same thing with God's financial success for our lives. We try to receive all His blessings down a very small avenue of income. We may wonder why more financial success has not come into our lives, yet perhaps we have allowed only one lane of blessing. Maybe God wants to send three, four, or even five lanes of financial abundance for us to use for His kingdom!

The promises of God are greater in scale than the volume of traffic on a Los Angeles freeway at rush hour. Too often we try to persuade God to send them down a small avenue, not realizing they will bottleneck and cannot get through. If we were able to expand our avenues of finance, we would see a great deal more traffic by way of the fulfilled promises of God.

God offers five different avenues of income and financial blessing for His people. Our responsibility is to make sure all five are open for His use. He can multiply whatever we give Him. It is through these avenues that God will channel blessings from the spiritual realm into the physical realm.

The Labor Avenue

The first kind of income comes from physical labor. Work is the cornerstone of God's financial plan for our lives. It will always be a part of what happens in our finances. Unfortunately, there are members of the Body of Christ who feel that they do not need to work. Such a response is disobedient to God's principles. Every household must work: "If anyone will not work, neither shall he eat" (II Thessalonians 3:10).

The need for human labor is not a result of the fall of humanity. Even in the perfect environment of the garden, Adam exerted effort. God placed him in the garden of Eden, "to tend and keep it" (Genesis 2:15). The Fall brought in the unfruitfulness and unproductiveness of work (see Genesis 3:17-19).

However, labor alone and by itself can generate only limited resources. Whatever work we do can be done to the glory of God (see I Corinthians 10:31 and Colossians 3:17). I can distinctly remember a minister one Sunday morning saying, "You know, it really doesn't make any difference what occupation you have in life." From one perspective he is right. As James 4:14 indicates, this life is as brief as a vapor. Eternity is so long, relatively speaking, that in one sense the kind of income we receive does not matter, as long as we have a healthy attitude toward God as we labor.

In another sense, what we do does matter. Many Christians, including myself, have received the impression that ambition in life may be hazardous to one's relationship with God. I have heard teaching indicating that any desire to improve my place in life is grounds for questioning whether or not I am truly saved. Spunk, get-up-and-go, and other ambitions make me suspect as a born-again believer, according to this inaccurate teaching.

Titus 3:14 reads, "And let our people also learn to *maintain good works*, to meet urgent needs, that they may not be unfruitful" (emphasis added). According to the original Greek, the phrase *maintain good works* refers to occupations. Titus was an overseer of churches on the island of Crete. Paul, who sent him, said in effect, "Titus, teach God's people to maintain good occupations." I can see here a responsibility for believers to maximize their abilities and even improve their vocation. For some people this growth will come about through further education and becoming more multi-talented. For others it may mean new responsibilities or new skills. Logic says that the better occupation I have and the more I improve myself, the more of this world's resources I will be able to draw in. With additional wealth, I can help meet an increased amount of urgent needs.

Today's world is full of pressing needs. People are starving for lack of food, and societies are crumbling for lack of moral fiber.

From God's point of view, the most pressing of all needs is the one with eternal consequences: People are going to hell because they have not put their trust in God's Son. He died for their sins. He even rose from the dead. The Bible says, "To as many as *received* Him, to them He gave the right to become the children of God" (John 1:12), emphasis added. If you haven't received Him, your eternity with God is not yet certain. You first must hear this good news about salvation. Romans 10:9 (NAS) states, "That if you confess with your mouth Jesus as Lord, " (and you can't lie to God—you have to mean it) "and believe in your heart that God raised Him from the dead, you shall be saved." Yet many of the world's unreached millions still have not heard the gospel once or known a Christian face to face. Of the 6,000 or so languages spoken by people groups in this world, only 2,000 or so have any portion of the Scripture translated into their language.

God's people need to maintain legitimate, good occupations so they can access as much of this world's resources as possible. Then they can direct a portion of those resources into ministry designed to meet pressing needs.

Let him who stole steal no longer, but rather let him labor, working with his hands what is good, that he may have something to give him who has need (Ephesians 4:28).

Diligence Required

As chapter 2 observed, Joseph participated in one of the largest transfers of wealth that has ever taken place on planet earth. Joseph literally experienced the wealth of the sinner being transferred to the righteous (see Proverbs 13:22). Joseph ended up with all the money from two countries, all the cattle, and all the land. In addition, virtually everybody worked for him. He was prosperous by anyone's standards. Today's equivalent would be for someone to have dominion over all the money in America and western Europe combined. It was an unbelievable amount of money.

Readers often overlook one part of Joseph's story. Each step of Joseph's financial increase involved physical labor. He received a huge revelation from God. He gained insight into grain prices for 14 years—7 of plenty, followed by 7 of famine. Still, he had to add something to this information. He could not idly sit by and wait for money to roll in.

Genesis 41:46 says Joseph "went throughout all the land of Egypt." Joseph had to prepare the granaries that were to hold these massive amounts of grain. The contents would later be sold at market prices and would bring in huge revenues. Before the incredible increase could occur, Joseph undoubtedly got up early many mornings and worked many late nights. He made long rides over hot dusty roads. He put in enormous effort during those seven years of plenty. Joseph's outward expression was in line with Proverbs 10:4: "He who has a slack hand becomes poor, but the hand of the diligent makes rich."

God Cares about Our Attitudes

Fruitful labor needs the right inward expression as well. Paul describes this attitude in Colossians 3:22-23: "...in sincerity of heart, fearing God. And whatever you do, do it heartily, as to the Lord and not to men."

One example comes from the days of King Solomon. "The man Jeroboam was a mighty man of valor; and Solomon, seeing that the young man was industrious, made him the officer over all the labor force of the house of Joseph" (I Kings 11:28). One quality of Jeroboam's work received mention; he was industrious. I presume Jeroboam made extra effort. If something needed to be done, Jeroboam made it happen. He took initiative and got the job done. Solomon promoted him because of his industriousness.

This giant advancement opportunity was only the beginning, however. Somebody Else was also planning a new responsibility for Jeroboam:

Now it happened at that time, when Jeroboam went out of Jerusalem, that the prophet Ahijah the Shilonite met him on the way; and he had clothed himself with a new garment, and the two were alone in the field. Then Ahijah took hold of the new garment that was on him and tore it into twelve pieces. And he said to Jeroboam, "Take for yourself ten pieces, for thus says the Lord,

the God of Israel: 'Behold, I will tear the kingdom out
of the hand of Solomon and will give ten tribes to you'"
(I Kings 11:29-31).

God used a prophet to declare that Jeroboam will be
king over ten tribes. Perhaps this new role stemmed from
his quality of being industrious. First, peers commended
him; following that, God promoted him and made him ruler.
It is regrettable that Jeroboam did not maintain his walk
with the Lord in the years afterwards.

A person's faithfulness also will often lead to new
challenges. Many times these heavier responsibilities lead
to increased income. However, human labor is only the beginning of the ways in which God can bring financial increase into our lives.

The Avenue of Creativity and Resourcefulness

A second avenue of income involves creativity and
resourcefulness. It enables someone to find a need and fill
it. It may mean inventing a new product or service. Or it
can be used to improve an existing idea or concept.

Some time ago I was talking with a pastor who had
gotten a bit behind on his tax bill. He prayed for help to pay
his obligation. Because of his petition, he heard the voice
of the Lord. He heard a benediction through that window,
clearly and distinctly: "Use what you've got."

His response was the same as most people's. "What
do I have?" he asked God. The Holy Spirit's words reminded
him of the registered female dog his family owned. This
particular breed of dog could bear puppies that sell for $250

after they were weaned. He knew what the Lord was saying. They needed a large, healthy litter of puppies.

The female dog conceived and they were blessed with a good litter of nine healthy pups. Once weaned, each puppy sold for $250 each. Not only did the pastor have the money to pay the taxes, but he also had money left over. God's nature is to do "exceeding abundantly" above all that we ask or think (Ephesians 3:20 KJV).

Why did he not think of the idea before? As Paul said about his knowledge of God's love, "For now we see in a mirror, dimly..." (I Corinthians 13:12). God's benediction illumines things that are presently dim. I believe God helps us see more clearly how to make extra income. We learn how to add to our existing stream of income.

I ministered at another church in Kansas and heard a report about a man who started understanding something about God's benediction and the windows of heaven. He worked for a large manufacturer. The company had a program where they paid employees for ideas that helped the company save money. Understanding the meaning of benediction, he prayed, "Lord, show me how this company can save money in its operations."

He, of course, earned an hourly wage. On at least three different occasions God showed him ways to help the company save money. On one occasion he received $10,000 in addition to his wage. In another instance he gained an extra $7,000. A third instance brought him $5,000.

Not everyone works for a company that pays cash incentives for ideas. The point is that God's benediction generates creativity or resourcefulness. Those tools can help create a larger stream of income, either in your present vocation or separate from it.

The Avenue of Buying and Selling

I refer to a third kind of income as buying and selling. I explained this concept in chapter 4. I believe the best summary appears in Luke 19:13: "...Buy and sell with these while I go and return" (AMP). The stewards in this parable understood this activity as a normal, legitimate avenue of profit. They realized that prices fluctuate. Large-scale economic forces regularly drive various assets to undervalued prices.

The parable of the merchant in Matthew 13:45-46 talks about an undervalued asset. "The kingdom of heaven is like a merchant seeking beautiful pearls, who, when he had found one pearl of great price, went and sold all that he had and bought it." Presumably, this merchant knew pearls. He found probably the finest pearl he had ever seen. Amazingly, the price was affordable, perhaps because of being undervalued. (I believe the pearl was extremely undervalued since the merchant took an unusual step— he sold everything he owned to raise money.) He took a calculated risk because of his eagerness to obtain the precious commodity while it was still available. Jesus does not continue the story any further, because His point is to show how valuable the kingdom of God is. In other circumstances, however, a merchant finding an undervalued resource knows that if he can secure the funds to buy it, he will later double, triple, or possibly quadruple his fortune.

Believers have two distinct advantages over the world. First, as we grow in Christ, we are being delivered from fear and greed, the two emotional forces that drive the world financially. Second, the Holy Spirit working in us tells us of things to come (see John 16:13). Buying and selling can release additional funds into our lives and give us more opportunity to take dominion over our financial future.

The Avenue of Miracles

I call the fourth avenue of income miraculous provision. For example, imagine someone praying, "Lord, we need an extra $50 this week," and then receiving an unexpected offer for overtime at work. That answer came through the first avenue—labor. Remember the pastor who needed funds to pay his tax bill and the Lord spoke to him, "Use what you've got"? His answer to prayer came through the avenue of creativity and resourcefulness. The third avenue, buying and selling, may likewise come in answer to prayer, such as the previously mentioned retired missionary who bought undervalued Hummel figurines.

This fourth avenue represents divine provision, independent and apart from any other source. God shows Himself in this way, I believe, simply to remind us that He is still God.

For instance, when Peter needed to pay his taxes, the Lord said to him, "I want you to go fishing. The first fish that comes up, I want you to take the gold coin out of its mouth" (see Matthew 17:27). That was miraculous. Peter had caught a lot of fish, but this was his first to have a gold coin in its mouth. His efforts were minimal in light of the provision.

This miraculous provision still happens today. He likes to demonstrate that He is God of gods and Lord of lords.

The Avenue of Inheritance

We play a passive role in this fifth avenue. It involves income or other resources that we inherit. Most of the decisions are in the hands of God and others.

It is Scriptural to pass wealth to succeeding generations. The Bible tells us that Abraham gave all that he had to Isaac (see Genesis 25:5). Isaac was able to start at a great place. He could start where Abraham stopped. Proverbs 13:22, the same Scripture that says the wealth of the sinner is laid up for the righteous, also says, "A good man leaves an inheritance to his children's children."

There is a problem with the way people today handle inheritances. It appears that when people leave their estate to their offspring, they often have not trained those offspring how to handle money. Children receive little training at school about handling money. They probably receive minimal training at church about handling money either. All of a sudden, they have dumped in their lap more money than they have ever had at any one time. Statistics indicate that for most people, the money disappears in six months to a year with very little to show for it.

In Bible times, parents would start passing out the inheritance before they died. This enabled them to instruct

117

their children on how to handle the money. They were there, if mistakes arose, to give advice. This helped the children prepare to deal with money on a larger scale. The same was sometimes true with the grandchildren. What if, in keeping with Proverbs 13:22a, every generation prepared for their grandchildren as well?

Each generation would then get money when needed. When could a family use some inheritance? How about when we start "buying" our newborn back from the hospital? If grandparents begin preparing for their grandchildren, each generation will get a financial boost at a crucial time.

We can leave our posterity an inheritance without leaving them an actual estate. We can teach them that there are ways to go through life with either low debt or no debt. We can teach them how to budget and make wise purchases. That legacy would be worth more than any dollar amount we leave behind. Our children and grandchildren may even be spared some of the struggles that we went through.

God can and will use inheritance as a means of bringing financial dominion into our lives. It begins with financial wisdom, but includes estates planned to bring us provision and blessing.

Converging Streams

God intends, at different points in time for different people, several if not all five of these streams of income to start flowing together to create a large river. This convergence is exactly what happened to King Solomon.

The weight of gold that came to Solomon yearly was six hundred and sixty-six talents of gold, besides that from the traveling merchants, from the income of traders, from all the kings of Arabia, and from the governors of the country (I Kings 10:14-15).

Solomon received a certain amount of tax revenue, just as any sovereign would, whether he was wicked or wise. What distinguishes Solomon is what he added to his revenue. Solomon received God's wisdom and benediction through the open windows (see I Kings 3:4-5). This word positioned him to do personal consultation for kings, queens, and nobles (see I Kings 10:1-10, 24-25). His revenue increased as a result.

I Kings 10:28-29 says that Solomon bought horses and chariots and sold them to some heathen kings—again, another increase. Solomon had access to resources beyond the ordinary person. However, the point is not where we are, but in which direction we are headed. God told Solomon he would "rise above the kings" (I Kings 3:13, my paraphrase). He rose above his peers; we will do the same. If you are a carpenter, you will rise above the other carpenters; if you are a salesperson you will rise above your peers.

Another example comes from the life of the virtuous woman of Proverbs.

Who can find a virtuous wife? For her worth is far above rubies. The heart of her husband safely trusts her; so he will have no lack of gain. She does him good and not evil all the days of her life. She seeks wool and flax, and willingly works with her hands. She is like the merchant ships, she brings her food from afar. She also rises while it is yet night, and provides food for her household, and a portion for her maidservants. She considers a field and buys it; from her profits she plants a vineyard. She girds herself with strength, and strengthens her arms. She perceives that her merchandise is good, and her lamp does not go out by night. She stretches out her hands to the distaff, and her hand holds the spindle. She extends her hand to the poor, yes, she reaches out her hands to the needy. She is not afraid of snow for her household, for all her household is clothed with scarlet. She makes tapestry for herself; her clothing is fine linen and purple. Her husband is known in the gates, when he sits among the elders of the land. She makes linen garments and sells them, and supplies sashes for the merchants (Proverbs 31:10-24).

This woman combined several streams of income and followed a simple step-by-step process. Over a period of time it brought her into a nice income. Initially she was not desperate for income. Her husband was a community leader; he was probably financially set in his own right (see verse 23). It is safe to assume that their household already had plenty of money.

The virtuous woman had a foundation for success—she was a giver (v. 20). Malachi's principle teaches that God will pour out a benediction through the open windows. The moment this woman started giving, the windows opened and the benediction started flowing. We can assume that God is saying something that fits her perfectly.

She wanted to create income in her own right. Thus, she set out on an ingenious strategy. In verse 13, we find she seeks wool and flax and works willingly with her hands. This virtuous woman saw a need in the marketplace and moved to meet it. She starts making some garments and offers them for sale in the local marketplace.

Imagine how this may have happened. Perhaps she was down in the market shopping for a dress for her little girl. While looking at the dresses, she says, "I cannot believe this. There's not but $2 worth of material in this and they want $20 for it." She may have thought, "I could do that." So she bought some wool and flax and started making garments to sell in the market.

She created a stream of income; now she faces a choice. No doubt she wanted some things. She may have wanted new clothes or new furniture. However, if the virtuous woman took all of the money she was earning and bought everything she wanted, she would forfeit her right to get to the next financial level. So I believe she temporarily puts her desires on hold.

There are points in our lives when delayed gratification will yield greater future blessing. They do not wait forever; only temporarily. The virtuous woman had a stream of money coming in and instead of spending it on the things her flesh wanted, it seems that she allowed that money to pool up. She also began learning about investments of a larger nature.

Next she created an additional stream of income. She considered a field and bought it. From her profits (verse 16) she planted a vineyard. What profits? These were the profits she got from her labor—those garments she put up for sale in the local marketplace. One day she noticed a field outside town that was a worthy investment and started a vineyard. Now she can sell the grapes and the fruit of the vine.

In addition to all that, she started yet another stream of income. Foreign merchants began to take the virtuous woman's garments to other cities, and possibly other countries. (In verse 24, *merchant* actually means Canaanite.) The wealth of the wicked was coming to the righteous. She simply continued to expand her stream of income.

I observe several important principles in what she apparently did. First, because she was a giver, she tapped into the benediction and moved to meet a need. God said something that fit her life perfectly. She created a stream of income. Next, instead of spending all that money to satisfy her personal desires, she let that money pool up and learned about bigger investments. She learned about fields and vineyards. She learned about what she could do if she made that kind of investment. Therefore, she created a different stream of income. Finally, merchants took her garments to different regions. This account in Proverbs 31 probably represents a few years' time.

Now the virtuous woman can probably buy many of the things she wanted and still keep her businesses going. She could still keep extending her hands to the poor. I like verse 18: "She senses that her gain is good" (NAS). What a wonderful sense that must be!

In following her example, suppose I put 40 hours a week into my job. I need to budget my money in a way that this income will meet my basic needs. My next move is to link my skills and abilities with a divine benediction in order to create an additional stream of income. This will require a few hours each week. I must temporarily put on hold the desire to spend that extra money on all the things I would like to have. I need to allow some of these funds to accumulate. The accumulation period allows me to learn about investments or bigger projects. This will generate a second stream of income. You can follow this pattern and continue stepping up.

I heard from a sister in Iowa who personally lived out a financial improvement similar to the virtuous woman. This woman was similar to most of us in that she held employment 40 hours a week and her job did not provide an overflowing blessing. She benefited from a creative idea. When she saw a need for additional food service in the downtown business area, she secured a food cart to service this need. Then she employed a teenager to handle the food cart, and so created a stream of income. Later she spotted an opportunity in the rental market. Her community had suffered during the agricultural and real estate downturn of the 1980's. As her money pooled, she was able to purchase a small rental house at a very good price. This extra stream built itself so she bought a second rental home. An addi-tional stream of income came as she bought quilts in the Midwest for $100-$125 and sent them to an aunt in California who sold them for $400-$600. With all those streams converging, she was able to enjoy that overflowing blessing.

In Summary

The essence of how our Christianity is to be expressed in the world appears in Mark 10:42-45. As with all Biblical principles, it is not quick, but the results are long-term.

But Jesus called them [the disciples] to Himself and said to them, "You know that those who are considered rulers over the Gentiles lord it over them, and their great ones exercise authority over them. Yet it shall not be so among you; but whoever desires to become great among you shall be your servant. And whoever of you desires to be first shall be slave of all. For even the Son of Man did not come to be served, but to serve, and to give His life a ransom for many (Mark 10:42-45).

The essence of Christian living resides in serving as many people as possible. Jesus taught that if we desire to become great, we should put our effort into serving others.

When I made the decision to go into a traveling field ministry from the pastorate, I did so because it was the best way to serve the Body of Christ at that point in my life. I asked myself, "How could I best serve Christ's church at this time?" I made my decision based on how I could best serve, unaware of what the financial consequences would be. It took a period of a few months, but my income soon became greater than before. I had no idea what to expect financially. Money was certainly not my motivation because some people I knew in field ministry had not done well financially!

In the earliest days of my travels, I offered each church the opportunity to make free copies of my outline available to those attending the meeting. Most churches did not take the time or the expense to make the copies. I would go to a meeting, and no notes would be available. People had nothing to study after I left. I saw a need for workbooks, so I began making outlines available at a nominal cost. As I moved to serve a legitimate need, my income went up again.

I once had a lady come to me and say, "I notice you don't have any tapes." I responded that I had thought people could simply obtain them from their church. She said, "It takes our church two weeks or longer sometimes to duplicate tapes. I would like to hear the tapes again now. I have some friends who need to hear the tapes now. If you had tapes on your table, I would buy at least two or three sets from you." There was a need. I started making tapes available. I moved to meet a specific need, but my income increased again.

I had been traveling for slightly more than a year when a little boy asked about an outline for his mother. He said she could not afford to buy it so I gave him the outline as a gift. A month after that happened, I was preparing for a service when the Lord reminded me of that incident. He made me aware of the fact that those who need this material the most are often the ones who can afford it the least. I sensed His will was to ask people in that position to give what they could toward the suggested price. I asked those who were presently abounding with finances to give a little extra.

This proposition took all the faith I could muster! I obeyed and put the idea into practice. Remarkably, my income went up again. Some did accept my offer and gave a nominal amount toward the teaching tapes. There were more individuals, however, who gave above the suggested price. Two results occurred due to this change: I was able to meet more needs and at the same time I saw my income rise.

If Christians live their lives focused on serving needs the Lord lets them see, the final yield will be far more than we can imagine. Servanthood is the key to causing all of the five streams of revenue to flow together in our lives. Servanthood brings dominion over our finances and allows us to use His resources to meet the greatest need of all—reaching the lost with the gospel.

Questions

1. Identify the parts of your current money stream according to the categories described in this chapter. Which has the likelihood of greatest potential increase?

2. Which Scripture cited in this chapter took on fresh meaning?

3. Why is servanthood so central to the Christian faith?

Key Action Points:

I. Recognize that there are multiple streams from which you can gain revenue
II. If you are employed by someone, increase your value to your employer - as well as saving money from your wages that you can use to increase
III. Examine your attitudes and motives

Chapter 7

Biblical Financial Cycles

Most of life tends to operate on some kind of cycle. Nature is full of cycles that are essential to human survival. Water falls from the sky and brings refreshment. Eventually it evaporates. Moisture in the air then gathers into clouds and falls as rain or snow. The process of this cycle meets the water needs for all life on the planet. It also purifies the water through its various stages. Without this cycle, we would be in danger of extinction. Nature, as established by God, is wonderful in its completeness.

God uses other kinds of cycles to bring financial completeness to His people. These cycles are incredibly important for any Christian's long-term finances. In order to experience lasting financial freedom, a believer must learn to understand and flow with Biblical financial cycles.

The apostle Paul talks about the two segments of this financial cycle. In most cases, every believer will travel

travel through both phases of it. Here is his teaching:

> *I have learned in whatever state I am, to be content: I know how to be abased, and I know how to abound. Everywhere and in all things I have learned both to be full and to be hungry, both to abound and to suffer need. I can do all things through Christ who strengthens me. Nevertheless you have done well that you shared in my distress. Now you Philippians know also that in the beginning of the gospel, when I departed from Macedonia, no church shared with me concerning giving and receiving but you only. For even in Thessalonica you sent aid once and again for my necessities. Not that I seek the gift, but I seek the fruit that abounds to your account. Indeed I have all and abound. I am full, having received from Epaphroditus the things sent from you, a sweet-smelling aroma, an acceptable sacrifice, well pleasing to God. And my God shall supply all your need according to His riches in glory by Christ Jesus* (Philippians 4:11b-19).

In this passage, Paul said that he knew how to live in two different financial climates. In verse 12 he says, "I know how to be abased, and I know how to abound...." When the apostle Paul said, "I know how," I believe he was not merely speaking about a natural knowledge that comes from his own experience. He was also speaking about revelation knowledge that comes from the heart of God.

The time of abasing can occur for various reasons but the net evidence is the same: finances fall off. Virtually every Christian has known a time of abasement.

Paul also turns the picture around and mentions a time of financially abounding. Money becomes abundant and exceeds what we need.

Tight Finances May Indicate a Time of Sowing

Paul said he knew how to be content in both positions. He knew what to do when his finances became restricted. He also was able to handle more wealth than he needed. His words demonstrate that there is an appropriate response to each phase of the cycle.

I believe that times of abasing and abounding are actually another way to depict seed time and harvest. Harvest time occurs when you reap grain or gather produce. Everything is in abundance. Seed time is just the opposite. The farmer has gone through the winter and must use his or her reserve of grain to plant in the ground. Farmers plant the seed in anticipation of a harvest in the upcoming months. Seed time is actually a phase of abasing.

The question we each need to ask ourselves is, "Do I know in my spirit what I should do when my finances are abased, and do I have a revelation from God of what I should do when my stores of material wealth abound?" Too often we believers walk in carnal human knowledge of what we should do. I believe it is possible to step out of that natural framework and into Holy Spirit-given knowledge.

At some point in the future, your finances will encounter restrictions. It is inevitable. However, this time of abasing may not be as deep as what you have experienced in the past. You may be facing persecution or a new life stage when your base income changes, such as at retirement. These chapters in your life are exceptions to the rule. Remember too, as the Foreword to this book observes, there are exceptional people "of whom the world was not worthy" (Hebrews 11:38), those like the Lord Jesus who had "nowhere to lay His head" (Matthew 8:20).

Barring events like these exclusions, you will tend to have both higher highs and higher lows. That is, your abasing will represent a time that is lower than the last previous high.

Almost nothing climbs in a perfectly direct line. No financial market, no business, and no economy ever rises in a consistently straight line. However, when looking at the big picture over time, you can and should see an overall upward trend.

When Financial Abasement Calls

Many different factors can restrict or abase your finances. One possibility is an attack of the devil. The devices of the enemy include fiery darts (see Ephesians 6:16). In John 10:10 Jesus says, "The thief does not come except to steal, and to kill, and to destroy. I have come that they may have life, and that they may have it more abundantly."

The believer's enemy is a thief. Without a doubt, Satan delights in keeping a dedicated believer crippled in his or her finances. Financial bondage limits participation in the advance of the Kingdom of God. Therefore, there are moments when my finances are restricted simply because I find myself under a full-scale attack of the enemy.

Transition is another primary cause of abasing. Transition occurs when God moves us from one station in life to another. For instance, He may be taking you from one kind of ministry or vocation into another.

When God shifts us from one ministry or vocation to another, He often desires to make us better off in the long run. However, in that initial and comparatively short transition period, our finances may face restraints. For instance, I was a pastor for eight years. During that time our congregation gave me a salary that I received on a regular basis. When God directed me into field ministry, I experienced a transition. During this time my income was somewhat below what I had received as a pastor. I realized this was just a transition, though; it was not His primary intention to reduce my finances. He had moved me, first to be a more effective servant of the Body of Christ. Second, He also chose to position me so that I would be better off financially.

Perhaps you presently work for someone else. A day may come when the Lord will let you know in your heart that it is His will for you to go into business for yourself. If so, you will probably face a period of time in which your finances are restricted. Predictably, the early days of becoming established will most likely not yield the level of income potential you now enjoy. He is positioning you where you will have more finances and can begin to do the things you hold in your heart for the Kingdom of God and for your family. The abasing is usually temporary.

Perhaps you will decide to get more training so that you can advance in your job or even get a better position. Your employer may pay for a portion of this schooling, but you may have restricted finances for a period of time if you pay for some or all of this training. Again, this is a type of voluntary abasing—but once you have the training and your employer promotes you or gives you a new position with a higher salary or more opportunity, you can begin to abound.

These circumstances show why it is so important to lower any personal debt. If I am living in a way that takes every dime of present income just to pay the bills, God might need to leave me where I am. Any transition to a better opportunity with initially lower income or higher expenses may do unacceptable harm. I might get behind on my obligations, which could put more pressure on me than what I could withstand. My debt may actually limit His options for me. Even the children of Israel limited God (see Psalm. 78:41). What an amazing thought: my actions can end up limiting what God would like to do in my personal life. Debt may even limit my ministry opportunities.

Learning to Be Content

It is tough to think of most situations of abasement in a positive sense. The Apostle Paul viewed it both spiritually and victoriously. He said, "I know how to be abased" (Philippians 4:12). He seems to speak with a confidence and conviction.

Paul said, "I have learned to be content whatever the circumstances" (Philippians 4:11 NIV). Spiritually minded people can learn how to be content with what God is presently providing. They know that He does not intend to leave us abased permanently. The abasing time compels us to focus on our priorities. It presses us to sharpen our prayer life and become tuned up spiritually.

It is no secret that we can become lax in our priorities. Our prayer life can lose its cutting edge. We can pick up "baggage" and become involved in unproductive endeavors. Our thought life likewise can lose its balance. When our finances go through this restricting time, most believers decide, "I need to get into prayer and find out what's going on here. My finances aren't what they were a few months ago."

As prayer develops a new found fervency, we start focusing on what the Spirit of the Lord is trying to say to us. Our priorities come back in focus. We are in preparation for the abounding side of the cycle.

The Apostle Paul explained what to do when facing abasement. "I can do all things through Christ who strengthens me" (Philippians 4:13). He made that statement in direct reference to facing abasing and abounding. I am to stop relying on my own natural strength and step into the strength of the Lord Jesus. I will draw on the life God has placed in me through the new birth. I will get to know Him better.

There is one thing we should not do during abasement. We must not spend our time grumbling. Complaining will only spiritually worsen our situation. Perhaps our whining will even prolong this period of abasement.

An important question to ask when finances are restricted is, "Lord, what am I supposed to learn in this situation that will strengthen me spiritually, and make me more like Jesus? What am I supposed to learn that will make me a better steward when my finances abound?" I believe this attitude will help bring us out of a time of abasing much more quickly.

Suppose We Are Never Abased

One of the churches described in Revelation never benefited from a time of abasement.

So then, because you are lukewarm, and neither cold nor hot, I will vomit you out of My mouth. Because you say, "I am rich, have become wealthy, and have need of nothing"—and do not know that you are wretched, miserable, poor, blind, and naked—I counsel you to buy from Me gold refined in the fire, that you may be rich; and white garments, that you may be clothed, that the shame of your nakedness may not be revealed; and anoint your eyes with eye salve, that you may see (Revelation 3:16-18).

They failed to allow God to reshape them. Therefore they ended up in a very sad spiritual condition. The biggest mistake the people in this church made was to say in their hearts, or even with their mouths, "I have need of nothing." They had allowed themselves to become independent from God. What a dangerous state!

The constant abounding blinded the members of the Laodicean church. They grew lukewarm in their relationship with God. Jesus recognized that they did not know how desperate their condition really was. He told them to repent and restore godly priorities. He challenged them to anoint their eyes and see from a true perspective. He wanted them to recognize that they needed God.

I heard a compelling analogy concerning sheep many years ago. The Bible frequently refers to believers as sheep. Jesus is the Chief Shepherd. He is the Good Shepherd of the sheep (see John 10:11). When sheep abound, as it were, their coat of wool is beautiful, soft, and fluffy. It looks good for a while. However, there comes a point when, if the wool continues growing thicker and thicker, it gets dirty. It captures thorns and thistles. That beautiful coat becomes dirty and disgusting. If the sheep were to fall into a pond or a lake, the wool would absorb the water. It would become so heavy that the sheep would probably drown.

Therefore sheep need shearing for their own good. The shepherd will remove most of that coat of wool. In one sense, the sheep may hate to lose the wool. In another, it feels free and clean. Now the sheep is ready to grow an entirely new coat of wool.

The same is true with believers. At times we can get a little dirty as we abound, figuratively speaking. Our spiritual wool can become cluttered with things that are not supposed to be there. The Good Shepherd may then come along and make a transition in our lives.

Through the time of abasement we find courage to refocus on our priorities and put them in order. Often we need to have our lives and attitudes cleaned out through a time of heart searching. Only then are we ready to resume that upward trend.

When God Calls You to Abundance

Abundance comes from several sources. Sometimes God gives it as a reward for our faithfulness to Christ. Proverbs 28:20a reads, "A faithful man will abound with blessings." The stewards who multiplied their master's talents in Jesus' parables received more as their reward.

Another cause of abundance is our financial seed growing up. These tithes and offerings can ripen to be a good, bountiful crop. II Corinthians 9:6 reads, "But this I say: He who sows sparingly will also reap sparingly, and he who sows bountifully will also reap bountifully." God enables us to harvest the seed we have sown.

Whatever the source, God's abundance allows us to do things for Him that were previously not possible with restricted finances. If I am in a time of abounding and my church wants to go on a missions trip that costs $700 per person, I can participate in these types of projects. I also can help people in ways I was not able to do so before. Maybe I can underwrite someone else's costs. Or perhaps, I can take some time away from my work and give a hand when I could not otherwise.

For a number of years, I was privileged to be the pastor of one sister from Missouri. This woman worked at a manufacturing company. She saw that the manufacturer was laying off people and consolidating many of its operations. She knew that a day could come when her job might not be available to her.

Following the leading of the Holy Spirit, she started a cleaning business of her own. She worked at her regular job as well as in this extra business she had started. God started blessing her business. She began making more in the cleaning business than she was on her job. When the manufacturer cut her job back, she was prepared. She had seen ahead of time.

Ultimately, her regular job was phased out. She expanded her business and her income remained abundant.

There will be times when the Lord Jesus will guide us (see John 16:13). He often lets us know of something coming up ahead so we can prepare. We can foresee the evil and do something about it (Proverbs 27:12). This sister did exactly that. The overall situation provided extra income.

As this sister's income grew, she began to go on missions trips to one of the Caribbean islands. She would teach at some churches, lead ladies' Bible study groups, and minister the life of God to spiritually hungry people.

I have thought about her situation and realized that her time of abounding is allowing her to do things she could not previously do. She now has the money to go when God leads her to go. She is able to take time off from her business when God directs. These are some of the wonderful benefits of this time of abounding.

I believe the time of abasing will usually be relatively short in duration. The time of abounding, I believe, has the potential to last much longer.

Responding to Abundance

Abundance is the fun time. That is when the financial seeds we have planted begin to bring a harvest. It is a very satisfying time. We have come through the time of transition; God has been moving in our lives. We have received more finances than what we need. Now we can support Kingdom values as never before.

God, knowing the fallen nature of humanity, warns us of attitudes to avoid during times of abundance. For example, we may be tempted to conclude, "I've got lots of money coming in; we could buy this or that on credit." Avoid the trap of accumulating heavy debt.

Otherwise, what will happen if the Spirit of God brings a change in your life and you go through a period of abasing? What if He calls upon you to do something different and beyond what you are now doing? Your heavy debt will drag you down. "The borrower is servant to the lender" (Proverbs 22:7 NIV). In fact, try to reduce debt as much as possible, especially try to eliminate the uncollateralized kind represented by charge cards and revolving charge accounts. Remember the siphon hose in your back pocket that I described in chapter 2!

Further, avoid the tug of materialism with its consumptive lifestyle. Keep your priorities in line, even as your standard of living goes up along the way. When you make major purchases, such as a new house, car, or appliance, be careful not to do anything that will crowd the percentage that should go to the Lord.

Also wait for the leading of the Holy Spirit. Over time, you may find yourself seeking God with these questions: "Is it time for our family to move up?", "Is the Holy Spirit saying to us that it's time to move into a larger house?", or "Is it time for our family to upgrade our vehicle?" If the Holy Spirit is not leading you to buy a car, the last thing you want to do is walk through the car lots. At the right time, then move forward confidently. Buy the car. Buy the house. In the process, however, do not allow the devourer to take some of the harvest God has so graciously brought into your life. Stewardship means being responsible.

Invest for Future Turns of the Cycle

Another step to take at this time is to invest for increase. After you have given generously to the Lord's work, you will still have extra money above and beyond your necessities. Use the increase of those funds as did the wise stewards commended in Jesus' parables. Opportunities will come across your path. A piece of property you know is undervalued may come up for sale. Perhaps you know of a stock that is undervalued and expected to increase.

Use some of your abundance of money to prepare for the next side of the cycle. As the Scripture says, "Go to the ant, you sluggard! Consider her ways and be wise, which, having no captain, overseer or ruler, provides her supplies in the summer, and gathers her food in the harvest" (Proverbs 6:6-8).

The ant gathers food in the harvest when it is plentiful. It eats what is needed and stores the rest. It knows the harvest will not last forever; winter is coming. The ant sees through the false security of, "I don't need to set anything aside; there's plenty of provision around."

Winter does arrive. No food exists for the ant outside the mound. The ant does not worry though; it has something set aside. Neither is it afraid to use its reserves, for the ant knows winter will not last forever. Harvest is coming and food will again be plentiful.

We can imitate the ant. We must take advantage of the reaping season. Harvest will not last forever. A day will come when winter will blow on us. The seasons will change. During the time of abundance, we should lay up reserves for the time when the cycles change once again.

Should the change take place, we must not be afraid to use our reserves. Sometimes Christians become overly protective of our savings. We fail to use them as God intended because we are afraid of the future. The winter cycle will also come to an end. Harvest time is coming. When we need to, we must be willing to carefully draw down those reserves. The wise individual knows there are times of both abasing and abounding. There is seed time and harvest. "There is desirable treasure, and oil in the dwelling of the wise, but a foolish man squanders it" (Proverbs 21:20).

When to Hang On, When to Quit

Times of abasing can raise great doubts. Maybe we have stepped into a business venture or ministry project that does not seem to be coming together. The pieces do not fit. We need a guideline that helps us know when to let something go, when to change our strategy, or when to stay in there and stick with it.

Christians can have trouble, even when they are in the center of the will of God, such as the spiritual pruning of John Chapter 15. Even the Lord Jesus Himself went through times of temptation. Or we can experience trouble when we are away from God's will. Sometimes our own sin brings calamity. However, difficulty alone does not reveal God's will.

How can I know which of these applications fits my present situation? Only the Lord can tell us which is happening. An experience in Peter's life is instructive:

Now in the fourth watch of the night Jesus went to them, walking on the sea. And when the disciples saw Him walking on the sea, they were troubled, saying, "It is a ghost!" And they cried out for fear. But immediately Jesus spoke to them, saying, "Be of good cheer! It is I; do not be afraid." And Peter answered Him and said, "Lord, if it is You, command me to come to You on the water." So He said, "Come." And when Peter had come down out of the boat, he walked on the water to go to Jesus. But when he saw that the wind was boisterous, he was afraid; and beginning to sink he cried out, saying, "Lord, save me!" (Matthew 14:25-30)

A number of years ago I heard a minister teach on this topic and it stuck with me. When the disciples saw Jesus walking on the sea, they became scared. They were afraid He was a ghost. However, Peter took drastic action. Peter stepped out to do something he had never done before. For a little while, Peter also walked on the water.

There are two reasons Peter could get out of the boat. First, he had a word for it. Jesus had said, "Come." Second, Peter could see Jesus in the plan. Whenever we face a situation that is not going as well as it ought to be, and we are uncertain of God's direction, we need to consider these two issues. If we will ask ourselves the following two questions, they will settle it for us every time.

1. Do I have a word for it? Is there a moment I can go back to when, definitely and beyond any shadow of a doubt, the Spirit of the Lord spoke to me or impressed me, and led me to do what I am doing? If so, we have satisfied the first half of the test.

2. Can I see Jesus in it? Is the hand of God a part of this project? Are His purposes being fulfilled? Am I behaving the way He would if this were His undertaking? If the answers are in the affirmative, keep on persevering. Do not quit now! Keep walking on the water.

In some instances you may find yourself frustrated, unable to think of an exact point when the Lord led you to do the project. Perhaps you are out there on your own. If you cannot see Jesus in it, my advice to you is return to the boat as fast as possible. Whatever it takes, swim, dog paddle, or float yourself back to the boat. Climb in it and seek after God's timing and benediction.

On the other hand, if you have received a word of confirmation, and if you can see Jesus in it, you need to continue to stand. Strengthen your shield of faith, knowing that it will quench every fiery dart the wicked one throws your way. In this case, you know you can walk on water and will keep walking on water. You will make it. You will be victorious. You will be the head and not the tail. You will be above and not beneath (see Deuteronomy 28:13).

In Summary

Foolproof Finances is a book designed to bring hope. I have met too many believers who have given up hope that their financial station in life will ever change. If their focus is on money alone, God may never entrust greater riches to them. However, any disciple of Jesus Christ can appropriate greater income for kingdom purposes. But there is a condition. That condition is that the person be willing to make foundational spiritual changes, both external and internal. Then after the proper turnaround takes place, any disciple of Christ can find great benefit from observing how Bible characters handled money. He or she can also receive a specific leading from God, a "benediction" on how best to apply talents, circumstances, and other God-given resources.

I have seen some phenomenal results in people's finances over several years of traveling ministry. It has been a privilege to share with the Body of Christ things that God has made very real to me. Apparently, the Holy Spirit has made them real to many other people as well. I have seen people's finances turn around. I have seen others make some Holy Spirit-sanctioned investments and prosper greatly. Some people have started actual businesses. The secret is to put the truth into practice.

I believe that the things you have learned in this book have the potential to alter the course of your life financially. God wants to use these truths to speak a word, a benediction, to your heart. God's Word will never fail. As you act on these truths, God will bring more finances into your life than you have experienced or seen up to this point. Remember, God wants to multiply your financial supply in order to further His Kingdom. As you practice these principles, eternity will be impacted by your faithfulness to God.

Appendix A:

Tools for Money Management

Victory in budgeting will go a long way toward turning your finances around. But the right tools are essential.

There are many spiritual and natural reasons to bring divine order to your finances. For example, Luke 16:11 reads, "Therefore if you have not been faithful in the unrighteous mammon, who will commit to your trust the true riches?" In essence, why would God entrust believers with spiritual riches if we do not obey Him in how we use earthly riches?

The Right Tools Are Essential

Sometimes I try to perform repair tasks around the house. It provides a real sense of accomplishment when I succeed. The right tool designed for the job gives me confidence to begin. It makes the job simple. Actually, having the right tools can make anyone look like a veritable genius.

Money management does not have to be hard if someone just explains how to use some simple tools. I want to make you aware of some of the most common "tools" used to balance a family budget. You do not need to pass a complex "balanced-budget amendment." But you should understand the process and with the help of the Holy Spirit have some determination to "Just do it!"

You Need A B_ _ _ _ _

Sometimes we'd rather not even hear or say the "B" word. Many people cringe at the word *budget* because they think it is a task that forever nags, "Spend less, spend less." However, a budget can also guide us to spend more (especially men) on important investments like our family. (You know, some of us men are so tight that we squeak when we walk.) Sometimes a budget disciplines us to spend the same amount, but with different priorities. Sometimes it helps us with the best timing of when to spend.

The bottom line on budgeting is that it helps us resolve a very important issue. "I will not spend more than God is presently providing." This is the key to both getting out of debt and staying out of debt. Size of income is irrelevant. Whether you make $10,000 per year or $100,000 per year, if you spend 10% or 20% more than you make, you are headed for trouble! As is pointed out in chapter 2, using the verse from Haggai 1:6, if you have a hole in your money bag, you will end up with nothing left no matter how many dollars you pour into the top.

Overspending or an out-of-control budget is usually not due to the size of your income. I had a friend tell me his personal story which I believe you will find helpful. He was spending a little more than his income. Of course, he felt a pay raise would solve the problem. A raise came, and he still spent more than he made. Again the assumption, I'm not making enough! He was fortunate to receive another salary increase. Still, he spent more than his pay. Do you see a pattern?

My friend eventually realized the overspending was not caused by lack of pay: it was caused by (gasp!) a character flaw. If overspending continues to grow in proportion to pay increases, the problem gets gradually worse.

A budget is merely a plan for how to spend money. It can and should be flexible. It is not set in "concrete," nor is it equal to the Ten Commandments (irrevocable). Rather, it is a guide like the fuel gauge in your car; it lets you know if you have enough gas to reach your intended destination.

No normal person would set off to drive through the desert with a broken fuel gauge and no map. That would be suicidal! Yet financial landscapes can be just as harsh and unfriendly. Like the desert, vultures are waiting to pick your bones clean. Perhaps some of them are circling already!

By comparison few people would say that their chosen destination is bankruptcy or more debt. Few people want to experience increased stress and financial pressure. Yet that is where they are headed. A budget is an essential ingredient to reaching a new destination: financial freedom. This financial freedom can and should glorify God.

Smart Budgeting

Smart budgeting "...is built by wise planning, becomes strong through common sense, and profits wonderfully by keeping abreast of the facts" (Proverbs 24:3-4 TLB).

Many people think they budget if they regularly monitor their checkbook balance. That data is often misleading. Suppose, for instance, that you've just paid your rent or mortgage and your checkbook register indicates that you have a balance of $600 left. You may be misled into thinking you have a lot of available cash. In reality, you may need $100 for groceries, $75 for the electric bill, $200 for your car payment, $100 for your child's scout camp, and $75 for an upcoming dental appointment. As a result you actually had only $50 available for spontaneous spending. A workable budget provides a first line of defense against everything from false assumptions to flaky schemes.

Even a well educated person can have financial troubles. I recall hearing of a believer with a college degree, who was short of money to buy food for his family. He asked his pastor for help and was instructed to bring in his checkbook and bank statements. Amazingly, this brother had not balanced his checkbook for several months.

The pastor sent this individual to a church member who worked at a local bank so that he could have help in working through the statements and finding his true bank balance. Upon completion of this task, this man discovered that he had several hundred more dollars than he thought. One day he cannot buy food, the next day he has a surplus! His problem was not too little money; it was not keeping abreast of the facts.

The Budget Process

You can create a very helpful, basic budget by dividing it into parts or steps:
- Determine monthly income
- Allocate income to meet your expenses

Married people will plan a better budget if they complete the following exercise together.

STEP ONE: Write down your monthly income from all sources. Describe it and then indicate a dollar amount.

Example:

Wages: husband's job $X,XXX
            wife's job $X,XXX

Here are some ideas for income categories to use:
Wages
Salaries
Commissions/Tips
Rental Income
Other:
Other:

STEP TWO: Write down all your monthly expenses. Also include seasonal expenses and semi-annual bills divided down to show as a monthly expense.

Victory Hint: Some people may find it helpful to keep a record of all expenses for a couple of months. Doing so enables them to document what they actually spend for items such as food, gasoline, clothing, and recreation.

Examples:

Fixed Expenses
Tithes
Emergency Savings
Retirement Savings
Housing: Rent or Mortgage
Auto Loan
Credit Card Payoff
Property Taxes
Insurance
Other Taxes

Variable Expenses (Average)
Offerings
Utilities:
> Electricity
> Natural Gas
> Garbage
> Phone

Gasoline
Car Repairs & Maintenance (Hint: Over long
> periods of time this usually averages out
> to about what you spend on gasoline.)

Food
Household Supplies
Christmas and Birthdays
Recreation and Entertainment
Vacations
Clothing
Pocket Money for Discretionary Spending
Other:
Other:
Other:

Be as specific as possible. Instead of labeling a huge category as "Miscellaneous," divide it into measurable groups like "Postage," "Eating Out," and "Household Supplies." Otherwise, a lot of money can disappear as a discretionary expense.

Farms, businesses, and self-employed people have unique situations. Account for them. When you estimate, be conservative. Deduct business expenses before listing income in your personal budget.

Once you have established the numbers, begin asking the following questions.

1. Do expenses exceed income?
If so, prioritize expenses. What can be trimmed or delayed? For example, could you eat out less? Curtail recreation? Car Pool? Give up the daily paper? Disconnect cable television? Walk or ride a bike to work?
2. Are you getting value for the money you are spending?
Check out library books on the best buys in insurance, consumer goods, etc...
3. Your tithe should come first. Plan for & pay all mandatory expenses next. Then allocate money to discretionary expenses.
4. Discretionary expenses, especially miscellaneous spending money, must be watched carefully. Break down your monthly figure in to how much you can spend each week. If you ever spend over the amount that you've allocated for any expense, it must come out of another category or you will lose ground rapidly.
5. Make up a sheet each month that states how much you can/will spend on each category. A simple legal pad works just fine. As you spend money or write checks, deduct the

appropriate amount from each category. Each week, or as often as you like, add up the unspent total from each category. The total unspent money should equal the balance in your checkbook. The two numbers should match; if not, adjustments need to be made. Remember: never, never, never spend out of your checkbook. Spend from your budget page.

6. Let me suggest a couple of ways to deal with such expenses as recreation, miscellaneous, gasoline, etc.

A. The envelope system-

Each pay period deposit appropriate amounts into designated envelopes marked with the name of that expense. Spend for that category only out of its envelope. When the money is gone from any envelope, stop spending for that category.

B. For quarterly, semi-annual, & annual expenses - Consider depositing the appropriate amount each pay period into a savings or money market account. When those bills come due, withdraw the money and pay the bills.

7. If expenses still exceed income, can mandatory expenses by restructured?

8. If expenses cannot be brought into line with your income, you should seek counsel with your pastor or an elder in your church as to what your next step should be.

9. During the budgeting process, husband and wife must communicate regularly. It takes approximately 6 months to become comfortable with living on a budget.

This process may result in some changes. Some people may need to begin some long-term restructuring. For instance, maybe you bought a house or a car beyond what your income will allow. Perhaps, you can also reduce inappropriate or duplicate insurance coverage. Maybe you should raise insurance deductibles.

Victory Hint: Look around for qualified individuals who can advise you. Make an appointment to talk with an economically stable family in your church who has already fought and won the "battle of the budget." Their advice and encouragement will be a great asset to you.

STEP THREE: Experiment, learn, and grow with your budget. Keep revising it until it works for you. Whether you keep the budget in your checkbook, on a computer spreadsheet or financial program, or on a ledger book, continue to tweak your system. When you can end a month with a money cushion to spare, you know that you are making tremendous forward progress.

Be sure to celebrate victories. When a credit-card debt gets paid off, do something fun to honor the occasion. Treat yourself and your family to ice cream sundaes, dinner out, or something special. Do not demand immediate perfection from yourself. Be aware that some months will be harder and others easier.

Money management for a Christian is not a mechanical exercise. It involves spiritual changes as God reveals character flaws you need to address. Remember that He wants you to win. He loves you dearly and cares deeply about every part of your life. With God's grace and help, a budget can help position you to receive both spiritual riches and material increase.

You can win the "battle of the budget" starting today. Victory is within your grasp. Budgeting may seem like a "bear", but remember this: David had to slay the bear before he could slay the giant. For you, greater victories lie ahead.

Scripture References

158

You can do better financially!

Why Starve to Death in a Supermarket: The Biblical Road to Increasing Your Finances a series of eight one hour audio or video lessons by author and financial advisor David Mallonee. Just for a set of eight audio tapes on finances a secular publisher could easily charge you $199. But Kingdom offers you financial information backed up by the Bible at an affordable price - only $40 for eight audio cassettes. Eight one hour videos lessons are available for only $29.95 each or the complete set of eight video lessons for only $97 + $5 shipping.

If you want this teaching on both audio and video cassettes- you can have both sets for only $119.95 + $7 shipping. Listen in your car and watch at home.

Credit Card Orders may call toll free 1-800-334-1456

Why Starve to Death in a Supermarket: The Biblical Road to Increasing Your Finances:
Eight audio cassettes #KPTWS8   *Only* $40 + $2 shp

Eight video lessons #KPVMFS   *Only* $97 + $5 shp

Both sets audio and video #KPTVWS only $119.95 +
$7 shp

Or send check, money order, or credit card # & expiration date along with cardholder signature to:
Kingdom, Inc.
P.O. Box 486
Mansfield, PA 16933

Free Information

Kingdom Computers

Kingdom offers personal computer systems for churches, Christian families, businesses, and schools. Some of the nations leading colleges and universities have labs full of Kingdom Computers. If you would like more information on Kingdom Computers, you may call toll free for a free computer catalog.

Call toll free 1-800-488-1122
Local number or from outside the U.S. (717) 662-7515
Fax (717) 662-3875
or write: Kingdom Computers
P.O. Box 486
Mansfield, PA 16933
internet: http://www.kingdominc.com/

Free Information for Cassette Ministries

Kingdom Tapes & Electronics

If you would like more information on cassette ministry supplies for your church such as high speed cassette duplicators, blank cassettes, microphones, and even church sound systems - call for the Kingdom Tapes & Electronics free catalog.

Call toll free 1-800-788-1122
Local number or from outside the U.S. (717) 662-7515
Fax (717) 662-3875
or write: Kingdom Tapes
P.O. Box 486
Mansfield, PA 16933
internet: http://www.kingdominc.com/

You can be part of the Story of Kingdom, Inc.

Kingdom, Inc. is a rapidly growing company located in North Central Pennsylvania. Kingdom's remarkable growth is attributable to the Lord's blessing and its Biblical operating principles. To learn more about Kingdom, read the Foreward to this book.

Perhaps you can become part of the Kingdom story. Expectations for continued growth at Kingdom is high. The talented team of employees is highly dedicated to Kingdom and its mission. If Kingdom sounds like it might be a good match for you and your talents, feel free to mail us your resume'.

Kingdom, Inc.
Attn: Personnel Dept. FFDM
P.O. Box 486
Mansfield, PA 16933

For published products, Kingdom is now looking for individuals who believe that the Lord has called them to bring a message to His church. If you are on a mission to bring a message God has given you for His church and are already successfully bringing this message to the church on a local or regional basis we'd like to hear from you. Just place Attn: Chief Editor on correspondence.

Free Financial Cassette

Free Cassette by David Mallonee. If you enjoyed this book, you'll love hearing David Mallonee on audio cassette. This free cassette is a one hour introduction to David's audio series: *Why Starve to Death in a Supermarket: The Biblical Road to Increasing Your Finances*. This cassette will help you do better financially.

Just drop us a note. Feel free to tell us what you thought of this book. Just enclose $1.25 for shipping and handling to receive your free cassette. Request *Foolproof Finances* free cassette offer: #KPFCDM1. Don't forget- David would love to hear your comments on this book.

Write: Kingdom, Inc.
P.O. Box 486
Mansfield, PA 16933